Richard Baxter, Alexander Balloch Grosart

What We Must Do to Be Saved

Richard Baxter, Alexander Balloch Grosart

What We Must Do to Be Saved

ISBN/EAN: 9783337312800

Printed in Europe, USA, Canada, Australia, Japan

Cover: Foto ©Lupo / pixelio.de

More available books at **www.hansebooks.com**

THE GRAND QUESTION RESOLVED.

WHAT WE MUST DO TO BE

SAVED:

INSTRUCTIONS

FOR A

Holy Life.

BY

The late reverend Divine

MR RICHARD BAXTER.

Recommended to the Bookseller a few days before his death, to be immediately printed for the good of souls.

ACTS xvi. 30. Sirs! What shall I do to be saved?

LONDON:

Printed for THO. PARKHURST, at the Bible and Three Crowns, Cheapside. 1692. [12°]

Collation: Title-page and pp. 46.

THE GREAT CASE RESOLVED,

HOW TO BE CERTAINLY SAVED.

Instructions for a Holy Life.

I. THE NECESSITY, REASON, AND MEANS OF HOLINESS.
II. THE PARTS AND PRACTICE OF A HOLY LIFE.

For personal direction and for family instruction. With two short Catechisms and Prayers.

READER,

IGNORANT persons cannot remember long and many words, nor understand a brief style and few words. This maketh it impossible to write a Catechism that shall not be unsuitable either to the understanding or the memory of such. I must therefore desire the Teacher to make up the unavoidable defect, by opening the meaning,—especially of the Catechisms,—to the children and servants, when they have learned and say the words. Read the Instructions often to them and press all as you go, on their affections. For the bare words without a present guide may else be all lost.

I. The necessity, reason, and means of Holiness.
1. *To keep up the resolutions of the converted.* And
2. *To instruct those in families that need them.*

Though the saving of souls be a matter of inexpressible importance,* yet—the Lord have mercy upon them!—what abundance are there that think it not worthy of their serious enquiry, nor the reading of a good book, one

---

* Mark viii. 36: Matthew vi. 33: Job xxi. 14, and xxii. 17: Psalm i. 2, 3, and xiv. 12.

hour in a week! For the sake of these careless slothful sinners, I have here spoken much in a little room, that they may not refuse to read and consider so short a lesson, unless they think their souls worth nothing. Sinner! As thou wilt shortly answer it before God, deny not to God, to thyself and me, the sober pondering and faithful practising these few directions :—

I. Begin at home, and *know thyself.* Consider what it is to be a *man.** Thou art made a nobler creature than the brutes. They serve thee, and are governed by thee; and death ends all their pains and pleasures. But thou hast reason to rule thyself and them; to know thy God, and foresee thy end, and know thy way, and do thy duty. Thy reason, and free-will, and executive power, are part of the image of God upon thy nature: so is thy dominion over the brutes, as, under him, thou art their owner, their ruler, and their end. But thy holy wisdom, and goodness, and ability, is the chief part of his image on which thy happiness depends. Thou hast a soul that cannot be satisfied in knowing, till thy knowledge reach to God himself:† nor can it be disposed by any other; nor can it or the societies of the world, be well governed according to its nature, without regard to his sovereign authority and without the hopes and fears of joy and misery hereafter;‡ nor can it be happy§ in anything but seeing and loving and delighting in this God as he is revealed in the other world. And is this nature given thee in vain? If the nature of all things be fitted to its use and end,∥ then it must be so with thine.

II. By knowing thyself then, thou must needs know *that there is a God*:¶ and that he is thy maker and infinite in all perfections; and that he is thy Owner, thy Ruler

---

* Psalm viii. 4-6: Genesis i. 26, 27: ix. 6: Col. iii. 10.
† John xvii. 3: 1 John iv. 6, 7: Jeremiah ix. 24.
‡ Luke xii. 4, 5.   § Psalm xvi. 5-11.   ∥ Isaiah xlv. 18.
¶ Psalm xiv. 1: Genesis i. 1: Revelation i. 8: Romans i. 19, 20: Psalm xlvi. 10: ix. 10: c. and xxiii.: xix. 1-3: xlvii. 7: Ezekiel xviii. 4: Genesis xviii. 25: Malachi i. 6.

and thy Felicity or End. He is mad that seeth not that such creatures have a cause or maker: and that all the power and wisdom and goodness of the world, is caused by a power and wisdom and goodness which is greater than that of all the world. And who can be our Owner but he that made us? And who can be our highest Governor but our Owner, whose infinite power wisdom and goodness maketh him only fit thereto? And if he be our Governor, he must needs have laws, with rewards for the good and punishments for the bad; and must judge and execute accordingly. And if he be our chiefest Benefactor, and all that we have is from him, and all our hope and happiness is in him, nothing can be more clear than that the very nature of man doth prove that in hope of future happiness, he should absolutely assign himself to the will and disposal of this God, and that he should absolutely obey him,* and that he should love and serve him with all his power: it being impossible to love, obey and please that God too much who is thus our cause, our end, our all.

III. By knowing thus thyself and God, it is easy to know *what primitive holiness and godliness is*. Even this hearty, entire and absolute resignation of the soul to God, as the infinite power, wisdom, and goodness: as our Creator, our Owner, Governor, and Felicity or End: fully submitting to his disposal, obeying his laws, in hope of his promised rewards and fear of his threatened punishments: and loving and delighting in himself and all his appearances in the world: and desiring and seeking the endless right and enjoyment of him in heavenly glory, and expressing these affections in daily prayer, thanksgiving and praise. This is the use of all thy faculties, the end and business of thy life, the health and happiness of

---

* Matthew xxii. 37: Jeremiah v. 22: 2 Corinthians v. 8, 9: Titus ii. 14: 2 Corinthians viii. 5, and vi. 16–18: 1 Peter ii. 9: Psalm 10: xxxvii. 4: xl. 8: Colossians iii. 1, 2: Matthew vi. 20, 21: 2 Cor. iv. 17, 18.

thy soul. This is that holiness or godliness which God doth so much call for.

IV. And by this it is easy to know what *a state of sin and ungodliness is.** Even the want of all this holiness, and the setting of carnal self instead of God. When men are proudly great and wise and good in their own eyes, and would dispose of themselves and all their concernments, and would rule themselves and please themselves, according to the fleshly appetite and fancy: and therefore love most the pleasures and profits and honours of the world as the provision to satisfy the desires of the flesh: and God shall be no further loved, obeyed, or pleased than the love of fleshly pleasures will give leave, nor shall have anything but what the flesh can spare: this is a wicked, a carnal, an ungodly state; though it break forth in various ways of sinning.

V. By this, *experience may tell you that all men*†—yea all till grace renew them—are *in this ungodly miserable state:* though only the Scripture tells us how this came to pass. Though all are not fornicators nor drunkards nor extortioners nor persecutors nor live not in the same way of sinning; yet selfishness and pride and sensuality and the love of worldy things, ignorance and ungodliness are plainly become the common corruption of the nature of man; so that their hearts are turned to the world from God, and filled with impiety, filthiness and injustice; and their reason is but a servant to their senses; and their mind and love and lip is carnal;‡ and this carnal mind is enmity to the holiness of God, and cannot be subject to his law. This corruption is hereditary, and is become, as it were, a nature to us, being the mortal malady of all our natures. And it is easy to know that such an unholy, wicked nature, must needs be loathsome to God and unfit

---

* Psalm xiv: 1: Hebrews xii: 14: Romans viii. 12, 13: John iii. 34: v. 6: 1 John ii. 15, 16: Romans xiii. 14, 15: vi. 16: Luke xviii. 23: xiv. 26, 33.
† Romans iii: Psalm 14: Ephes. ii. 2, 3: Romans v. 12, 17, 39: John iii. 6.
‡ Romans viii. 5, 6, 7.

for the happy enjoyment of his love, either here or in the life to come :* for what communion hath light with darkness ?

VI. Hence then it is easy to see *what grace is needful to a man's salvation.* So odious a creature, such an unthankful rebel that is turned away from God and set against him, and defiled with all this filth of sin, must needs be both renewed and reconciled,† sanctified and pardoned, if ever he will be saved. To love God and be beloved by him and to be delighted herein, in the might of his glory, is the heaven and happiness of souls: and all this is contrary to an unholy state. Till men have new and holy hearts, they can neither see God nor love him nor delight in him nor take him for their chief content : for the flesh and world have their delight and love. And till sin be pardoned,‡ and God is reconciled to the soul, what joy or peace can it expect from him whose nature and justice engageth him to loathe and punish it ?

VII. And experience will tell you *how insufficient you are for either of these two works yourselves:* || *to renew your souls or to reconcile them unto God.* Will a nature that is carnal resist and overcome the flesh and abhor the sin which it most dearly loveth ? will a wordly mind overcome the world ? when custom hath rooted your natural corruptions, are these easily rooted up ? O how great and hard a work is it to cause a blind unbelieving sinner to set his heart on another world and lay up all his hopes in heaven, and to cast off all the things he seeth for that God, and glory which he never saw. And for a hardened, worldly, fleshly heart to become wise and tender and holy and heavenly, and abhor the sin which it most fondly loveth ! And what can we do to satisfy justice and reconcile such a rebel soul to God ?

VIII. Nature and experience having thus acquainted

---

* Psalm iv. 3 : 2 Corinthians vi. 14, 17.
† Psalm xxxii. 1, 2 : 1 Corinthians vi. 11 : Titus ii. 14 : iii. 5–7 : Hebrews xiv. 14 : Matthew v. 8.   ‡ Romans v. 1–3.
|| Psalm xcvii. 7, 8, 15 : 1 Corinthians ii. 11, 21: Hebrews xiv. 12 : 2 Peter i. 3.

you with your sin and misery, and what you want, will further tell you that *God* doth not yet deal with you according to your deserts.* He giveth you life, and time, and mercies, when your sins had forfeited all these. He obligeth you to repent and turn unto him. And therefore experience telling you that there is some hope, and that God hath found out some way of shewing mercy to the children of wrath, reason will command you to enquire of all that are fit to teach you what way of remedy God hath made known. And as you very soon discover that the religion of heathens and Mahometans is so far from shewing the true remedy that they are part of the disease itself: so you may learn that a wonderful Person † the Lord Jesus Christ, hath undertaken the office of being the Redeemer and Saviour of the world: and that he who is the eternal Word and Wisdom of the Father, hath wonderfully appeared in the nature of man, which he took from the virgin Mary, being conceived by the Holy Ghost: and that we might have a Teacher sent from Heaven ‡ infallibly and easily to acquaint the world with the will of God and the unseen things of life eternal: how God bare witness of the Truth by abundant, open and uncontrolled miracles:‖ how he conquered Satan and the world,§ and gave us an example of perfect righteousness ¶ and underwent the scorn and cruelty of sinners, and suffered the death of the cross as a sacrifice for our sins to reconcile us unto God: how he rose again the third day and conquered death, and lived forty days longer on earth, instructing his apostles and giving them commission to preach the Gospel to all the world, and then ascended bodily into heaven,

---

* Acts xiv. 27 and xvii. 24–28: Romans i. 19, 20: Romans ii. 4: Job xxxiii. 14–25: Matthew xii. 42, 43.
† Isaiah ix. 6, 7, and liii: John iii. 16, 19, and i. 3, 4, and iii. 2.
‡ John i. 18. ‖ Acts ii. 22: Hebrews ii. 3, 4. § Matthew iv.
¶ 1 Peter ii. 22–25: Matthew: xxvi. 27–28: Acts i.: Hebrews iv: Ephesians i. 22, 23: Romans v. 1, 3, 9: Hebrews viii. 9, 13, and viii. 6, 7: Hebrews vii. 25: 1 John v. 10, 12: John v. 22, and iii. 18, 19: Matthew xxv.

while they gazed after him : how he is now in heaven, both God and man in one Person, the Teacher and King and High-priest of his Church. Of him must we learn the way of life : by him must we be ruled as the physician of souls. All power is given him in heaven and in earth. By his sacrifice and merits and intercession must we be pardoned and accepted with the Father : and only by him must we come to God. He hath procured and established a covenant of grace, which baptism is the seal of: Even that God will in him be our God and reconciled Father, and Christ will be our Saviour, and the Holy Ghost will be our Sanctifier, if we will unfeignedly consent; that is if penitently and believingly we give up ourselves to God the Father, Son and Holy Ghost, in these resolutions. This covenant in the tenor of it is a deed of gift, of Christ and pardon and salvation to all the world : if by true faith and repentance they will turn to God. And this shall be the law according to which he will judge all that hear it at the last: for he is made the judge of all, and will raise all the dead, and justify his saints and judge them unto endless joy and glory, and condemn the unbelievers, impenitent and ungodly,* unto endless misery. The soul alone is judged at death, and body and soul at the resurrection. This Gospel the apostles preached to the world ; and that it might be effectual to man's salvation, the Holy Ghost was first given to inspire the preachers of it,† and enable them to speak in various languages, and infallibly to agree in One, and to work many great and open miracles to prove their word to those they preached to. And by this means they planted the Church;‡ which ordinary ministers must increase and teach and oversee, to the end of the world, till all the elect be gathered in. And the same Holy Spirit hath undertaken it as His work ‖ to accompany this Gospel and by it to convert men's souls,

---

* Luke xvi.   † Acts ii: John xvii. 23.
‡ Matthew xxviii. 19, 20: Acts xiv. 23: Acts xx: xxvi. 17, 18.   ‖ Romans viii. 9.

illuminating and sanctifying them; and by a secret regeneration * to renew their natures and bring them to that knowledge and obedience and love of God which is the primitive holiness for which we were created and from which we fell. And thus by a Saviour and a Sanctifier must all be reconciled and renewed that will be glorified with God in heaven. All this you may learn from the Sacred Scriptures which were written by the inspiration of the Holy Spirit† and sealed by multitudes of open miracles,‡ and contain the very image and superscription of God, and have been received and preserved by the Church as the certain word of God, and blessed by him through all generations, to the sanctifying of many souls.

IX. When you understand all this it is time for you to look home ‖ and understand now *what state your souls are in*. That you were made capable of holiness and happiness, you know: that you and all men are fallen from God and holiness and happiness unto self and sin and misery, you know: that you are so far redeemed by Christ, you know, as to have a pardoning and saving covenant tendered you, and Christ and mercy offered to your choice. But whether you are truly penitent believers and renewed by the Holy Ghost and so united unto Christ, this is the question yet unresolved, this is the work that is yet to do, without which there is no salvation, and if thou die before it is done, woe to thee that ever thou wast a man! Except a man be regenerated by the Spirit § and converted and made a new creature, and of carnal be made spiritual, and of earthly be made heavenly, and of selfish and sinful be made holy and obedient to God, he can never be saved, no more than the devil himself can be saved. And if this be so—as nothing is more sure— I require thee now, who readest these words, as thou regardest thy salvation, as thou wouldst escape hell-fire and

---

* Titus iii. 5, 6: John xiii. 5, 6. † 2 Timothy iii 16.
‡ Hebrews ii. 3, 4.   ‖ 2 Corinthians xiii. 5: Psalm iv. 4: 2 Peter i. 10.
§ John iii. 5: 2 Corinthians v. 17: Romans viii. 7–9: Philippians iii. 18–20.

stand with comfort before Christ and his angels at the last, that thou soberly consider whether reason command thee not to try thy state : whether thou art thus renewed by the Spirit of Christ or not,* and to call for help to those that can advise thee† and follow on the search till thou know thy case. And if thy soul be a stranger to this sanctifying work, whether reason command thee not, without any delay, to make out to Christ, and beg his Spirit, and cast away thy sins, and give up thyself entirely to thy God, thy Saviour and Sanctifier, and enter into his covenant, with a full resolution never to forsake him ; to deny thyself and the desires of the flesh and this deceitful, transitory world, and lay out all thy hopes on heaven, and speedily, whatever it cost thee, to make sure of the felicity which hath no end? And darest thou refuse this when God and conscience do command it? And further I advise you,

X. Understand how it is that *Satan hindereth souls from being sanctified*, that you may know how much to resist his wiles. Some he deceiveth by malicious suggestions that holiness is nothing but fancy or hypocrisy :‡ and if God and death and heaven and hell were fancies, this might be believed. Some he debaucheth by the power of fleshly appetite and lust, so that their sins will not let their reason speak : some he keepeth in utter ignorance by the evil education of ignorant parents and the negligence of ungodly soul-murdering teachers :∥ some he deceiveth by worldly hopes, and keepeth their minds so taken up with worldly things, that the matters of eternity can have but some loose and uneffectual thoughts, or as bad as none : some are entangled in ill company,§ so make a scorn of a holy life, and feed them with continual diversions and vain delights : and some are so hardened in their sin¶ that

---

* Acts xvi. 14.
† Acts ii. 37, and xvi. 30, and xi. 33 : 2 Corinthians vi. 1, 2 : Rev. ii. 7.
‡ Acts xxiv. 14, and xxviii. 22, and xxiv. 5, 6.
∥ Malachi ii. 7–9 : Hosea iv. 9. § Proverbs xiii. 20.
¶ Ephesians iv. 18, 19.

they are even past feeling, and neither fear God's wrath nor care for their salvation, but hear these things as men asleep, and nothing will awake them. Some are discouraged with a conceit that godliness is a life so grievous,* sad and melancholy, that rather than endure it they will venture their souls, come on it what will—as if it were a grievous life to love God and hope for endless *joys;* and a pleasant life to love the world and sin, and live within a step of hell!—Some that are convinced do put off their conversion with delays, and think it's time enough hereafter: and are purposing and purposing till it be too late, and life and time and hope be ended.† And some that see there is a necessity of holiness are cheated by some dead opinion or names or shews and images of holiness:‡ either because they hold a strict opinion or because they are baptized with water and observe the outward parts of worship: and perhaps because they offer God a great deal of lip-service and lifeless ceremony, which never savoured of a holy soul. Thus deadness, sensuality, worldliness and hypocrisy do hinder millions from sanctification and salvation.

XI. If ever thou wouldest be saved, *oppress not reason by sensuality or diversions:* but sometimes retire for sober consideration.‖ Distracted and sleepy reason is unuseful. God and conscience have a great deal to say to thee: which in a crowd of company and business thou art not fit to hear. It is a doleful case§ that a man who hath a God, a Christ, a soul, a heaven, a hell to think of, will allow them none but running thoughts, and not once in a week bestow one hour in man-like serious consideration of them.¶ Sure thou hast no greater things to mind. Resolve then sometimes to spend half an hour in the deepest thoughts of thy everlasting state.

---

* Malachi i. 13. † Matthew xxv. 3, 8, 12, and xxiv. 43, 44.
‡ John viii. 39, 42, 44: Romans iii. 1, 2: Galatians iv. 29: Matthew xiii. 19–22, and xv. 2, 3, 6: Galatians i. 1.
‖ Psalm iv. 4: Haggai i. 5: Deuter. xxxii. 7–29. § Isaiah i. 3.
¶ Job xxxiv. 27: Jer. xxiii. 20: Psalm cxix. 59.

XII. *Look upon this world and all its pleasures as a man of reason, who foreseeth the end:* and not as a beast that liveth by sense or present objects.* Do I need to tell thee, man, that thou must die? Cannot carcases and dust instruct thee to see the end of earthly glory and all the pleasures of the flesh? Is it a controversy whether thy flesh must shortly perish? and wilt thou yet provide for it before thy soul? What a sad farewell must thou shortly take of all that worldlings sell their souls for! And O how quickly will this be! Alas! man, the day is even at hand: a few days more and thou art gone! and darest thou live unready, and part with heaven for such a world as this?

XIII. And then think soberly on the life to come:† what it is for a soul to appear before the living God and be judged to endless joy or misery! If the devil tempt thee to doubt of such a life, remember that nature and Scripture and the world's consent, and his own temptations are witnesses against him. O man canst thou pass one day in company or alone in business or in idleness, without some sober thoughts of everlastingness? Nothing more sheweth that the hearts of men are asleep or dead than that the thoughts of endless joy or pain, so near at hand, constrain them not to be holy and overcome not all the temptations of the flesh as toys and inconsiderable things.

XIV. *Mind well, what mind most men are of when they come to die!*‡ Unless it be some desperate forsaken wretch do they not all speak well of a holy life? and wish that their lives had been spent in the most fervent love of God and strictest obedience to his laws? Do they then speak well of lust and pleasures and magnify the wealth and honours of the world? Had they not rather die as the most mortified saints, than as careless, fleshly worldly sin-

---

* 2 Corinthians iv. 8: Deut. xxxii. 29: 1 John ii. 17: 1 Cor. vii. 31: Luke xii. 19, 20: John xiv. 1, 2: 1 Thess. v. 13.

† Luke xii. 4: Eccl. xii. 7: 2 Peter iii. 11: 2 Cor. iv. 18: Phil. iii. 18, 20.

‡ Numbers xxiii. 10: Matt. xxv. 8; vii. 21 22: Prov. i. 28, 29.

ners? and dost thou see and know this, and yet wilt thou not be instructed to be wise in time?

XV. *Think well what manner of men these were whose names are now honoured for their holiness.** What manner of life did St Peter and St Paul, St Cyprian, St Augustine, and all other saints and martyrs live? Was it a life of fleshly sports and pleasures? Did they deride or persecute a holy life? Were they not more strictly holy than any that thou knowest? And is he not self-condemned that honoureth the names of saints and will not imitate them?

XVI. Think what the difference is *between a Christian and an heathen.*† You are loath to be heathens or infidels. But do you think a Christian excelleth them but in opinion? He that is not holier than they, is worse, and shall suffer more than they.

XVII. Think what the difference is *between a godly Christian and an ungodly.*‡ Do not all the opposers of holiness among us yet speak for the same God and Christ and Scripture: and profess the same creed and religion, with those whom they oppose? And is not this Christ the author of our holiness, and this Scripture the commander of it? Search and see, whether the difference be not this, that the godly are serious in their profession, and the ungodly are hypocrites, who hate and oppose the practise of the very things which themselves profess: whose religion serveth but to condemn them while their lives are contrary to their tongues.

XVIII. Understand what the devil's policy is by *raising so many sects and factions and controversies about religion in the world :* ‖ even to make some think that they are reli-

---

* Matthew xxiii. 29-33: Heb. xi. 38: John viii. 39.
† Matthew x. 15: Romans ii: Acts x. 34, 35.
‡ Romans ii. 28, 29: Matthew xxv. 28: Luke xix. 22: Acts xxiv. 15: Galatians iv. 29.
‖ Ephesians iv. 14: Acts xx. 30: 1 Corinthians xi. 19: 2 Timothy iv. 3, and ii. 14, 16: 1 Timothy i. 5, 6: Titus iii. 9: Ephesians iv. 3 etc.: 1 Corinthians xii: Matthew xii. 25: Romans ii. 12, 27-29.

gious because they can prate for their opinions, or because they think their party is the best, because their faction is the greatest or the best; the uppermost or the suffering side. And to turn holy, edifying conference into vain jangling; and to make men atheists—suspecting all religion and true to none—because of men's diversity of minds. But remember that [the] Christian religion is but one, and a thing easily known by its ancient rule; and the universal church containing all churches, is but one. And if carnal interest or opinions so distract men that one party saith 'We are all the Church,' and another saith 'It is we' —as if the kitchen were all the house or one town or village all the kingdom—wilt thou be mad with seeing this distraction? Hearken sinner, all those sects in the Day of Judgment shall concur as witnesses against thee if thou be unholy : because however else they differed,* all of them that are Christians professed the necessity of holiness and subscribed to that Scripture which requireth it. Though thou canst not easily resolve every controversy thou may'st easily know the true religion, it is that which Christ and his apostles taught, which all Christians have professed, which Scripture requireth : which is first pure and then peaceable : † most spiritual, heavenly, charitable, and just.

XIX. *Away from that company ‡ which is sensual*, and an enemy to reason, sobriety and holiness, and consequently to God, themselves and thee. Can they be wise for thee that are foolish for themselves? or friends to thee that are undoing themselves? or have any pity on thy soul when they make a jest of their own damnation? will they help thee to heaven who are running so furiously to hell? Chuse better familiars if thou woulds't be better.

XX. *Judge not of a holy life by hearsay*, for it cannot so

---

* Galatians i. 7, 8 : Matthew xxviii. 20.   † James iii. 17.
‡ Ephesians v. 11: Proverbs xxiii. 20: 2 Corinthians vi. 17, 18: Psalm xv. 4: Deuteronomy xiii. 3.

B

be known.* Try it awhile and then judge as thou findest it. Speak not against the things thou knowest not. Hadst thou but lived in the love of God, and the lively belief of endless glory, and the delights of holiness, and the fears of hell but for one month or day : and with such a heart hadst cast away thy sin† and called upon God and ordered thy family in a holy manner, especially on the Lord's day, I dare boldly say experience would constrain thee to justify a holy life.‡ But yet I must tell thee it is not true holiness if thou but try it with exceptions and reserves. ‖ If therefore God hath convinced thee that this is his will and way, I adjure thee as in his dreadful presence, that thou delay no longer § but resolve, and absolutely give up thyself to God as thy heavenly Father, thy Saviour and thy Sanctifier, and 'make an everlasting covenant with him,' and then he and all his mercies will be thine : his grace will help thee and his mercy pardon thee : his ministers will instruct thee and his people pray for thee and assist thee : his angels will guard thee and his Spirit comfort thee : and when flesh must fail and thou must leave this world, thy Saviour will then receive thy soul and bring it into the participation of his glory : and he will raise thy body and justify thee before the world and make thee equal to the angels : and thou shalt live in the sight and love of God and in the everlasting pleasures of his glory. This is the end of faith and holiness. But if thou harden thy heart and refusest mercy ¶ everlasting woe will be thy portion, and then there will be no remedy.

And now, Reader, I beg of thee and I beg of God on my bended knees that these few words may sink into thy heart and that thou wouldest read them over and over again and bethink thee as a man that must shortly die.

* John v. 40: Luke xiv. 29, 30: John vi. 35, 37, 45.   † Isaiah lv. 6, 7.
‡ Matthew xi. 19.   ‖ Luke xiv. 33.
§ Revelations xxii. 17: John i. 12: Revelations ii. and iii. : 1 John v. 12, 13: Psalm xxxiv. 7: Psalm lxxiii. 26: Matthew xxv.: Luke xx. 39: Hebrews ii. 3: 1 Thessalonians ii. 12.   ¶ Luke xix. 27: Proverbs xxix. 1, and i. 10, etc.

Whether any deserve thy love and obedience more than God? and thy thankful rememberance more than Christ? and thy care and diligence more than thy salvation? Is there any felicity more desirable than heaven? or any misery more terrible than hell? or anything so regardable as that which is everlasting? Will a few days' fleshly pleasures pay for the loss of heaven and thy immortal soul? or will thy sin and thy prosperity be meet at death and in the day of judgment? If thou art a man, and as ever thou believest that there is a God and a world to come, and as thou carest for thy soul, whether it be saved or damned, I beseech thee, I charge thee, think of these things! think of them once a day at least! think of them with thy most sober, serious thoughts! Heaven is not a May-game and hell is not a flea-biting! Make not a jest of salvation or damnation! I know thou livest in a distracted world where thou mayest hear some laughing at such things as these, and scorning at a holy life, and fastening odious reproaches on the godly, and merrily drinking and playing and feasting away their time, and then saying that they will trust God with their souls and hope to be saved without so much ado! But if all these men do not change their minds and be not shortly down-in-the-mouth, and would not be glad to eat their words, and wished that they had lived a holy life, though it had cost them scorn and suffering in the world, let me bear the shame of a deceiver for ever. But if God and thy conscience bear witness against thy sin and tell thee that a holy life is best, regard not the gain-sayings of a bedlam-world, which is drunk with the delusions of the flesh. But give up thy soul and life to God by Jesus Christ in a faithful covenant! Delay no longer, man, but resolve, resolve immediately, resolve unchangeably: and God will be thine and thou shalt be his for ever. Amen. Lord have mercy on this sinner and so let it be resolved by thee in him.

II. The Parts and Practice of a holy life for personal

and family instructions. All is not done when men have begun a religious life.* All trees that blossom prove not fruitful, and all fruit comes not to perfection. Many fall off who seemed to have good beginnings; and many dishonour the name of Christ, by their scandals and infirmities. Many do grieve their teachers' hearts and lamentably disturb the Church of Christ, by their ignorance, errors, self-conceitedness, unruliness, headiness, contentiousness, sidings and divisions: insomuch that the scandals and the feuds of Christians are † the great impediments of the conversion of the infidel and heathen world, by the exposing Christianity to their contempt and scorn, as if it were but the error of men as unholy and worldly and proud as others, that can never agree among themselves. And many by their passions and selfishness are a trouble to their families and neighbours where they live. And more by their weaknesses and great distempers, are snares, vexations and burdens to themselves. Whereas Christianity in its true constitution is a life of such holy light and love, ‡ such purity and peace, such fruitfulness and heavenliness, as, if it were accordingly shewed forth in the lives of Christians, would command admiration and reverence from the world and do more to their conversion than swords or words alone can do: and it makes Christians useful and amiable to each other and their lives a feast and pleasure to themselves. I hope it may prove some help to those excellent ends and to the securing men's salvation, if in a few, sound experienced directions I open to you the duties of a Christian life.

I. *Keep still the true form of Christian doctrine, desire and duty, orderly printed on your minds:* ‖ that is, understand it clearly and distinctly and remember it, I mean the great

---

* 1 Corinthians i. 25: Hebrews iv. 1: 2 Peter ii. 22: 1 Corinthians iii.: Galatians iii. and iv.: Matthew xiii. 41, and xviii. 7.

† Philippians iii. 18, 19: Acts xx. 30.

‡ Matthew v. 16: 1 Peter ii. 18: 2 Corinthians i. 21.

‖ 2 Timothy i. 13, and iii. 7: Hebrews v. 12: Philippians i. 9: Romans xv. 14.

points of religion contained in Catechisms. You may still grow in the clearer understanding of your Catechisms, if you live an hundred years. Let not the words only but the matter, be as familiar in your minds as the rooms of your house are. Such solid knowledge * will establish you against seduction and unbelief and will be still within you a ready help for every grace and every duty, as the skill of an artificer is for his work. And for want of this when you come among infidels or heretics, their reasonings may seem unanswerable to you, and shake if not overthrow your faith. And you will easily err in lesser points and trouble the Church with your dreams and wranglings. This is the calamity of many professors, that while they will be most censorious judges in every controversy about Church-matters they know not well the doctrine of the Catechism.

II. *Live daily by faith on Jesus Christ* † *as the Mediator between God and you.* Being well-grounded in the belief of the Gospel and understanding Christ's office, make use of him still in all your wants. Think on the fatherly love of God, as coming to you through him alone : and of the Spirit as given by him your head : and of the covenant of grace as enacted and sealed by him : and of the ministry as sent by him : and of all times and helps and hopes as procured and given by him. When you think of sin and infirmity and temptations, think also of his sufficient, pardoning, justifying and victorious grace. When thou thinkest of the world, the flesh and the devil, think how he overcometh them. Let his doctrine and the pattern of his most perfect life, be always before you as your rule. In all your doubts and fears and wants go to him in the Spirit and to the Father by him and him alone. Take him as the root of your life and mercies, and live as upon

---

* Ephesians iv. 13, 14: Colossians i. 9, and ii. 2, and iii. 10: 1 Timothy vi. 4.
† John xvii. 3: Ephesians iii. 17, 18: Matthew xxviii. 19: Ephesians i. 22, 23, and iv. 6, 16: Romans v.: 2 Corinthians xii. 9: John xvi. 33: 1 John v. 4: Hebrews iv. 14, 16, etc.

him and by his life; and when you die resign your soul to him that they may be with him 'where he is and see his glory.' To live as Christ and use him in every want and address to God, is more than a general confused believing in him.

III. *To believe in the Holy Ghost as to live and work by him, as the body doth by the soul.** You are not baptized into his name in vain; † but too few understand the sense and reason of it. The Spirit is sent by Christ for two great works. 1. To the apostles and prophets to inspire them infallibly to preach the Gospel ‡ and confirm it by miracles and leave it on record for following ages in the Holy Scriptures. 2. To all his members ‖ to illuminate and sanctify them to believe and obey this sacred doctrine —beside his common gift to many to understand and preach it. The Spirit having first indited § the Gospel doth by it first regenerate and after govern, all true believers. He is not now given us for the revealing of new doctrines but to understand and obey the doctrine revealed and sealed by him long ago. ¶ As the sun doth by its sweet and discreet ** influence both give and cherish the natural life of things, sensitive and vegetative: so doth Christ by his Spirit our spiritual life. †† As you do no work but by your natural life you should do none but by your spiritual life. You must not only believe and love and pray by it, and manage all your calling by it: for 'holiness to the Lord' must be written upon all. All things are sanctified to you because you being sanctified to God devote all to him and use all for him; and therefore must do all in the strength and conduct of the Spirit.

---

* Galatians v. 16, 25. † Matthew xxviii. 19.
‡ John xvi. 13: Hebrews ii. 34.
‖ 1 Corinthians xii. 12, 13: Romans viii. 9, 13: John iii. 5, 6.
§ Spelled 'indicted.' G. ¶ 2 Timothy iii. 15, 16: Jude 19, 20.
** 'Well-timed' or provident. G.
†† Ezekiel xxxvi. 27: Isaiah xliv. 3: Romans viii. 1, 5: 1 Corinthians vi. 11: Zechariah xiv. 20.

IV. *Live wholly upon God as all in all:* * as the first efficient, principal dirigent † and final cause of all things. Let faith, hope and love be daily feeding on him. Let 'our Father which art in heaven' be first inscribed on your hearts that he may seem most amiable to you and you may boldly trust him, and filial love may be the spring of duty. Make use of the Son and the Spirit to lead you to the Father: and of faith in Christ to kindle and keep alive the love of God. God's love is our primitive holiness and especially called, with its fruits 'our sanctification' which 'faith in Christ' is but a means to. Let it be your principal end in studying Christ, to see the goodness, love and amiableness of God in him. A condemning God is not so easily loved as a gracious reconciled God. You have so much of the Spirit as you have love to God. This is the proper gift of the Spirit to all the adopted sons of God, to cause them with filial affection and dependance to cry 'Abba Father.' Know not, desire not, love not any creature but purely as subordinate to God. Without him, let it be nothing to you, but as the glass without the face or scattered letters without the sense or as the corps without the soul. Call nothing prosperity or pleasure but his love: ‡ and nothing adversity or misery but his displeasure and the cause and the fruits of it. When anything would seem lovely and desirable which is against him, call it 'dung.' ‖ And hear that man as Satan and the serpent § that would entice you from him; and count him but vanity, a worm and dust, that would affright you from your duty to him. Fear him much but love him more. Let love be the soul and end of every duty. ¶ It is the end and reason of all the rest: but it hath no end or reason but its object. Think of no other heaven and end and happiness of man but love

---

* 1 Corinthians x. 31: Romans xi. 36: 2 Corinthians v. 7, 8: 1 John iii. 1: Romans v. 1-3: Matthew xxii. 37: Ephesians i. 6: 2 Corinthians v. 19: Galatians iv. 4-6. † *Sic*: cf. Richardson under 'dirge, dirige.' G.
‡ Psalm xxx. 5, and lxiii. 3. ‖ Philippians iii. 7, 8.
§ Matthew xvi. 13. ¶ 2 Thessalonians iii. 5: 2 Corinthians xiii. 14.

the final act and God the final object. Place not your religion in anything but the love of God, with its means and fruits. Own no grief, desire or joy but a mourning, a seeking and a rejoicing love.

V. *Live in the belief and hopes of heaven, and seek it as your part and end;* and daily delight your souls in the forethoughts of the endless sight and love of God.* As God is seen on earth but as in a glass so is he proportionably enjoyed. But when mourning, seeking love hath done, and sin and enemies are overcome, and we behold the glory of God in heaven, the delights of love will then be perfect. You may desire more on earth than you may hope for. Look not for a kingdom of this world, nor for Mount Zion in the wilderness. Christ reigneth on earth—as Moses in the camp—to guide us to the Land of the promise. Our perfect blessedness will be when the kingdom is delivered up to the Father and God is all in all. A doubt, or a strange, heartless thought of heaven, is water cast on the sacred fire, to quench your holiness and your joy. Can you travel one whole day to such an end, and never think of the place that you are going to? which must be intended † in every righteous act—either notedly or by the ready unobserved act of a potent habit. When earth is at the best it will not be heaven. You live no further by faith, like Christians, than you either live for heaven in seeking it or else upon heaven in hope and joy.

VI. *Labour to make religion your pleasure and delight.* Look oft to God, to heaven, to Christ, to the Spirit, to the promises, to all your mercies. Call over your experiences, and think what matter of high delight is still before you, and how unseemly it is, and how injurious to your profes-

---

* Colossians iii. 1–4: Matthew vi. 19–21, 33: 2 Corinthians iv. 17, 18, and vii.: Luke xii. 20: Hebrews vi. 20: 1 Corinthians xv. 28: Ephesians iv. 6, and i. 23: Philippians iii. 18, 20: Psalm lxxiii. 25, 26: John xviii. 36.

† Psalm i. 2, 3: lxxxiv. 2, 10: lxiii. 3, 5: xxxvii. 4: xci. 19: cxix. 47, 70: Isaiah lviii. 14: Psalm cxii. 1: Romans xiv. 17, and v. 1, 3, 5: 1 Peter i. 8: Matthew v. 11, 12: Psalm xxxii. 11.

sion for one that saith he hopeth for heaven, to live as sadly as those that have no higher hopes than earth. How should that man be filled with joy, who must live in the joys of heaven for ever! Especially rejoice when the messengers of death do tell you that your endless joy is near. If God and heaven with all our mercies in the way, be not reason enough for a joyful life, there can be none at all. Abhor all suggestions which would make religion seem a tedious, irksome life. And take care that you represent it not so to others; for you will never make them in love with that which you make them not perceive to be delectable and lovely. Not as the hypocrite, by forcing and framing his religion to his carnal mind and pleasure: but bringing up the heart to a holy suitableness to the pleasures of religion.

VII. *Watch as for your souls against this flattering, tempting world:* * especially when it is represented as more sweet and delectable than God and holiness and heaven. This world with its pleasures, wealth and honours, is it that is put in the balance by Satan, against God and holiness and heaven: and no man shall have better than he chooseth and prefereth. The bait taketh advantage of the brutish part when reason is asleep: and if by the help of sense it get the throne, the beast will ride and rule the man: and reason becomes a slave to sensuality. When you hear the serpent, see his sting and see death attending the forbidden fruit. When you are rising look down and see how far you have to fall! His reason as well as faith, is weak, who for such fools-gawds as the pomp and vanities of this world, can forget God and his soul and death and judgment, heaven and hell, yea and deliberately command them to stand by. What knowledge or experience can do good on that man who will venture so much for such a world, which

---

* Galatians vi. 14: 1 John ii. 15, 16: James i. 27 and iv, 4, 5: 1 John v. 4, 5: Romans xii. 2: Galatians i. 4: Titus ii. 12: Matthew xix. 24: Luke xii. 16, 21 and xvi. 25: James i. 11 and v. 1, 2, 4: Luke viii. 14: Hebrews xi. 26.

all that have tried it, call vanity at the last? How deplorable then is a wordling's case! Oh fear the world when it smileth or seems sweet and amiable. Love it not if you love your God and your salvation.

VIII. *Fly from temptations and crucify the flesh and keep a constant government over your appetite and senses.** Many who had no designed, stated vice or worldly interest, have shamefully fallen by the sudden surprise of appetite and lust. When custom hath taught those to be greedy and violent, like a hungry dog or a lusting boar, it is not a sluggish wish or purpose that will mortify or rule them. How dangerous a case is that man in who hath so greedy a beast continually to restrain! that if he do but neglect his watch an hour, is ready to run him headlong into hell! Who can be safe that standeth long on so terrible a precipice? The tears and sorrows of many years may perhaps not repair the loss which one hour or act may bring. The case of David and many others, are dreadful warnings. Know what it is you are most in danger of: whether lust and idleness or excess in meats or drinks or play: and there set your strongest watch for your preservation. Make it your daily business to mortify that lust, and scorn that your brutish sense or appetite should conquer reason. Yet trust not purposes alone : but away from the temptation. Touch not, yea look not on the tempting bait: keep far enough off if you desire to be safe. What miseries come from small beginnings! Temptation leads to sin, and small sins to greater, and those to hell. And sin and hell are not to be played with. Open your sin or temptation to some friend, that shame may save you from danger.

IX. *Keep up a constant, skilful government over your passions and your tongues.*† To this end keep a tender

---

* Romans viii. 1, 13: Galatians v. 24: Romans xiii. 14: Galatians v. 17 : Jude 8, 23 : 2 Peter ii. 10 : Ephesians ii. 3 : 1 Peter ii. 11 : Matthew vi. 13 : xxvi. 41 : Luke viii. 13.

†James i. 19: iii. 17 : 1 Peter iii. 4 : Matthew v. 5 : Ephesians iv. 2, 3 : Colossians iii. 12.

conscience, which will smart when in any of these you sin. Let holy passions be well-ordered; and selfish, carnal passions, be restrained. Let your tongues know their duties to God and man* and labour to be skilful and resolute in performing them. Know all the sins of the tongue, that you may avoid them: for your innocency and peace do much depend on the prudent government of your tongues.

X. *Govern your thoughts with constant skilful diligence.* † In this, rigid habits and affections will do much by inclining them unto good. It's easy to think on that which we love. Be not unfurnished of matter for your thoughts to work upon: and often retire yourselves for serious meditation. Be not so solitary and deep in musings as to over-stretch your thoughts and confound your minds or take you off from necessary converse with others. But be sure that you be considerate and dwell much at home, and converse most with your consciences and your God, with whom you have the greatest business. Leave not your thoughts unemployed or ungoverned, scatter them not abroad upon impertinent vanities! O that you knew what daily business you have for them. Most men are wicked, deceived and undone, because they are inconsiderate and dare not or will not, retiredly and soberly use their reason: or use it but as a slave in chains in the service of their passion, lust and interest. He was never wise or good or happy, who was not soberly and impartially considerate. How to be good, to do good and finally enjoy good, must be the sum of all your thoughts. Keep them first holy, then charitable, clean and chaste. And quickly check them when they look towards sin.

XI. *Let time be exceeding precious in your eyes, and care-*

---

* James i. 26: iii. 5, 6: Psalm xxxiv. 13: Proverbs xviii. 21.
† Deuteronomy xv. 9: 2 Corinthians x. 5: Genesis vi. 5: Psalm x. 4, and xciv. 19: cxix. 113: Proverbs xii. 5, and xv. 26: Psalm cxix. 59: Proverbs xxx. 32: Jeremiah iv. 14: Deuteronomy xxxii. 29.

fully and diligently redeem it. * What haste doth it make! and how quickly will it be gone! and then how highly will it be valued when a minute of it can never be recalled! O what important business have we for every moment of our time, if we should live a thousand years! Take not that man to be well in his wits or to know his God, his end, his work or his danger, who hath time to spare. Redeem it not only from needless sports and plays and idleness and curiosity and compliment and excess of sleep and chat and worldliness: but also from the entanglements of lesser good which would hinder you from greater. Spend time as men that are ready to pass into another world, where every minute must be accounted for; and it must go with us for ever as we lived here. Let not health deceive you into the expectation of living long, and so into a senseless negligence. See your glass running and keep a reckoning of the expense of time: and spend it just as you would review it when it is gone.

XII. *Let the love of all in their several capacities, become as it were your very nature:* and doing them all the good you can be very much of the business of your lives. God must be loved in all his creatures, his natural image on all men and his spiritual image on his saints. Our neighbour must be loved as our natural selves, that is, our natural neighbour as our natural self, with a love of benevolence: and our spiritual neighbour as our spiritual self, with a love of complacence. In opposition to complacence we may hate our sinful neighbour, as we must ourselves, much more. But in opposition to benevolence we must neither hate ourselves, our neighbour or our enemy. O that men

---

* Ephesians v. 16: John xiv. 1, 2: Acts xvii. 21: 1 Corinthians vii. 29: 2 Corinthians vi. 2: John ix. 4: Luke xix. 42, 44: Psalms xxxix. 4: Matthew xxv. 10, 12.

† 1 Timothy i. 5, 6: Matthew xix. 19: Romans xiii. 10: 1 John i. 16: Ephesians iv. 2, 15, 16: Colossians ii. 2, and i. 4: 1 Timothy vi. 11: James iii. 17: Philippians ii. 1, 2: 1 Thessalonians iv. 9: John xiii. 35: Matthew v. 44, 45: 1 Corinthians xiii.: James iv. 11: Galatians vi. 10: Titus ii. 14: Philippians ii. 20, 21: Romans xv. 1, 3.

knew how much of Christianity doth consist in love and doing good. With what eyes do they read the Gospel who see not this in every page? Abhor all that selfishness, pride and passion which are the enemies of love: and those opinions and factions and censurings and back-bitings, which would destroy it. Take him that speaketh evil of another to you without a just cause and call, to be Satan's messenger, entreating you to hate your brother or to abate your love. For to persuade you that a man is bad is directly to persuade you so far to hate him. Not that the good and bad must be confounded: but love will call none bad without constraining evidence. Rebuke back-biters. Hurt no man and speak evil of no man; unless it be not only just but necessarily to some greater good. Love is lovely: they that love shall be beloved; hating and hurting makes men hateful. 'Love thy neighbour as thyself,' and 'do as thou wouldst be done by,' are the golden rules of our duty to men: which must be deeply written on your hearts. For want of this there is nothing so false, so bad, so carnal which you may not be drawn to think or say or do against your brethren. Selfishness and want of love do as naturally tend to ambition and covetousness, and thence to cruelty against all that stand in the way of their desires, as the nature of a wolf to kill the lambs. All factions and contentions and persecutions in the world, proceed from selfishness and want of charity. Devouring malice is the devilish nature. Be as zealous in doing good to all as Satan's servants are in hurting. Take it as the use of all your talents, and use them as you would hear of it at last. Let it be your business and not a matter on the by: especially for public good and men's salvation. And what you cannot do yourselves, persuade others to. Give them good books: and draw them to the means which are most like to profit them.

XIII. *Understand the right terms of Church-communion:* especially the unity of the universal church and the universal communion which you must hold with all the parts and the difference between the Church as visible and invisible. For want of these how woeful are our divisions! Read oft 1 Corinthians xii., and Ephesians iv. 1–17: John xvii. 21–23: Acts iv. 32; ii. 42: 1 Corinthians i. 10, 11, 13: iii. 3: Romans xvi. 17: Philippians ii. 1–4: 1 Thessalonians v. 12, 13: Acts xx. 30: 1 Corinthians xi. 19: Titus iii. 10: James iii.: Colossians i. 4: Hebrews x. 25: Acts viii. 12, 13, 37: 1 Corinthians i. 2, 13: iii. 3, 4: xi. 18, 21. Study these well. You must have union and communion in faith and love with all the Christians in the world. And refuse not local communion when you have a just call so far as they put you not on sinning. Let your usual meeting be with the purest church, if you lawfully may—and still respect the public good—but sometimes occasionally communicate with defective, faulty churches, so be it they are true Christians and put you not on sin: that so you may show that you own them as Christians, though you disown their corruptions. Think not your presence maketh all the faults of ministry, worship or people to be yours—for then I would join with no Church in the world. Know that as the mystical church consisteth of heart-covenanters, so doth the Church as visible consist of verbal-covenanters, which make a credible profession of consent: and that nature and scripture teacheth us to take every man's word as credible, till perfidiousness forfeit his credit: which forfeiture must be proved, before any sober profession can be taken for an insufficient title. Grudge not then at the communion of any professed Christian in the Church visible*—though we must do our part to cast out the obstinately impertinent by discipline: which, if we cannot do, the fault is not ours. The presence of hypocrites is no hurt but oft a mercy to the sincere. How small else would the Church seem in the world! Outward privileges

---

* Matthew xiii. 29, 41.

belong to outward covenanters and inward mercies to the sincere. Division is wounding and tends to death.* Abhor it if you love the Church's welfare or your own. 'The wisdom from above is first pure then peaceable.' Never separate what God conjoineth. It is the earthly, sensual, devilish wisdom which causeth bitter envying and strife and confusion and every evil word. 'Blessed are the peacemakers.'

XIV. *Take heed of pride and self-conceitedness in religion*†. If once you over-value your own understandings, your crude conceptions and gross mistakes will delight you as some supernatural light; and instead of having compassion on the weak, you will be unruly and despisers of your guides and censorious contemners of all that differ from you, and persecutors of them if you have power, and will think all intolerable that take you not as oracles and your word as law. Forget not that the Church hath always suffered by censorious, worldly professors on the one hand—and O what divisions and scandals have they caused!—as well by the profane and persecutors on the other. Take heed of both: and when contentions are afoot be quiet and silent and not too froward, and keep up a zeal for love and peace.

XV. *Be faithful and conscionable in all your relations.* Honour and obey your parents and other superiors. Despise not and resist not government. If you suffer unjustly by them, be humbled for those sins, which cause God to turn your protectors into afflictors. And instead of murmuring and rebelling against them, reform yourselves and then commit yourselves to God. Princes and pastors I will not speak to: subjects and servants and children, must obey their superiors as the officers of God.

---

* John xvi. 2: 1 Corinthians i. 10: Romans xvi. 17: James iii. 14-18.
† 1 Timothy iii. 6: Colossians ii. 18: 1 Corinthians viii. 1: iv. 6: 1 Timothy vi. 4: 1 Peter v. 5: James iii. 1, 17: Ephesians v. and vi.: Colossians iii. and iv.: Romans xiii. 1, 7: 1 Peter ii. 13, 15.

XVI. *Keep up the government of God in your families.** Holy families must be the chief preservers of the interest of religion in the world. Let not the world turn God's service into a customary, lifeless form. Read the scripture and edifying books to them; talk with them seriously about the state of their souls and everlasting life; pray with them fervently; watch over them diligently; be angry against sin and meek in your own cause; be examples of wisdom, holiness and patience; and see that the Lord's day be spent in holy preparation for eternity.

XVII. *Let your callings be managed in holiness and laboriousness.*† Live not in idleness; be not slothful in your work be you bound or free; in the sweat of your brows you must eat your bread, and labour the six days that you may have to give to him that needeth: slothfulness is sensuality as well as filthier sins. The body that is able must have fit employments as well as the soul, or else body and soul will fare the worse; but let all be but as the labour of a traveller, and aim at God and heaven in all.

XVIII. *Deprive not yourself of the benefit of an able, faithful pastor,*‡ to whom you may open your case in secret, or at least of a holy faithful friend: ‖ and be not displeased at their free reproofs. § Woe to him that is alone! How blind and partial we are in our own cause! and how hard it is to know ourselves without an able, faithful helper! You forfeit this great mercy when you love a flatterer, and angrily defend your sin.

XIX. *Prepare for sickness, sufferings and death.* ¶ Overvalue not prosperity nor the favours of man. If selfish man prove false and cruel to you, even those of whom you have deserved best, marvel not at it, but pray for your

---

* *Command* iv: Joshua xxiv. 15: Deut. vi. 6–8: Daniel vi.

† Hebrews xiii. 5: *Command* iv.: 2 Thessalonians iii. 10, 12: 1 Thessalonians iv. 7: 1 Timothy v. 13: Proverbs xxxi.: 1 Corinthians vii. 29.

‡ Malachi ii. 7.

‖ Ecclesiastes iv. 10, 11. § Proverbs xii. 1; xv. 30, 31: Hebrews iii. 13.

¶ Luke xii. 40: 2 Peter i. 10: Philippians i. 21, 23: Jeremiah ix. 4, 5: Matthew vii. 4, 5: 2 Corinthians v. 1–2, 4, 8.

enemies, persecutors and slanderers, that God would turn their hearts and pardon them. What a mercy is it to be driven from the world to God, when the love of the world is the greatest danger of the soul! Be ready to die and you are ready for anything. Ask your hearts seriously, what is it that I shall need at a dying hour? And let it speedily be got ready and not be to seek in the time of your extremity.

XX. *Understand the true method of peace of conscience:* and judge not the state of your souls upon deceitful grounds. As presumptuous hopes do keep men from conversion and embolden them to sin: so causeless fears do hinder our love and praise of God, by obscuring his loveliness: and they destroy our thankfulness and our delight in God, and make us a burden to ourselves and a grievous stumbling-block to others. The general grounds of all your comfort are (1) the gracious nature of God* (2) the sufficiency of Christ † and (3) the truth and universality of the promise ‡ which giveth Christ and life to all, if they will accept him. But this acceptance is the proof of your particular title, without which these do but aggravate your sin. Consent to God's covenant is the true condition and proof of your title to God as your Father, Saviour and Sanctifier, and so to the saving blessings of the covenant: which consent, if you survive, must produce the duties which you consent to. He that heartily consenteth that God be his God, his Saviour and Sanctifier, is in a state of life. But this includeth ǁ the rejection of the world. Much knowledge, and memory, and utterance, and lively affection, are all very desirable. But you must judge your state by none of these, for they are all uncertain. But 1. If God and holiness and heaven have the highest esti-

---

* Exodus xxxiv. 6.   † Hebrews vii. 25.
‡ John iv. 42: John iii. 16: 1 Timothy iv. 10: ii. 4: Matthew xxviii. 19, 20: Rev. xxii. 17: Isaiah lv. 1-3, 6, 7.
ǁ Luke xiv. 26, 33: 1 John ii. 15: Matt. vi. 19, 20, 21, 33: Colossians iii. 1, 2: Romans viii. 1, 13.

mation by your practical judgment, as being esteemed best for you : 2. And be preferred in the choice and resolution of your wills and that habitually before all the pleasures of the world : 3. And be first and chiefly sought in your endeavours : this is the infallible proof of your sanctification. Christian, upon long and serious study and experience I dare boldly commend these Directions to thee, as the way to God, which will end in blessedness. The Lord resolve and strengthen thee to obey them. This is the true constitution of Christianity : this is true godliness : and this is to be religious indeed : all this is no more than to be seriously such as all among us in general would prefer to be. This is the religion which must difference you from hypocrites, which must settle you in peace and make you an honour to your profession and a blessing to those that dwell about you. Happy is the land, the church, the family, which doth consist of such as these ! These are not they that either persecute or divide the church or that make their *religion* a servant to their policy, to their ambitious designs or fleshly lusts ; nor that make it the bellows of sedition or rebellion or of an envious hurtful zeal or a pistol to shoot at the upright in heart. These are not they that have been the shame of their profession, to hardening of ungodly men and infidels, and that have caused the enemies of the Lord to blaspheme. If any man will make a religion of or for his lusts : of Papal tyranny, or Pharisaical formality, or of his private opinions, or of proud censoriousness and contempt of others : and of faction and unwarrantable separations and divisions and of standing at a more observable distance from common professors of Christianity than God would have them, or yet of pulling up the hedge of discipline and laying Christ's vineyard common to the wilderness—the storm is coming when this religion founded on the sand will fall "and great will be the fall thereof." When the religion which consisteth in faith and love to God and man, in mortifying the flesh and crucifying the world, in self-denial, humility and patience in sincere obedience and faithfulness in all relations, in watchful self-government, in doing good and in a divine and heavenly life, though it will be hated by the ungodly world—shall never be a dishonour to your Lord nor deceive or disappoint your soul.

A SHORT CATECHISM.

Quest. 1. What is the Christian Religion?

Ans. The Christian Religion is the baptismal-covenant made and kept: wherein God the Father, Son and Holy Ghost, doth give Himself to be our reconciled God and Father, our Saviour and Sanctifier: and we believingly give up ourselves accordingly to Him, renouncing the "flesh, the world and the devil." Which covenant is to be oft renewed, specially in the sacrament of the Lord's Supper.

Quest. 2. Where is our covenant-part and duty fuller opened?

Ans. 1. In the Creed, as the sum of our belief.
  „ 2. In the Lord's Prayer, as the sum of our desires.
  „ 3. And in the Ten Commandments (as given us by Christ, with the Gospel-explanations) as the sum of our practice. Which are as followeth—

THE CREED.

I believe in God the Father Almighty, Maker of heaven and earth; and in Jesus Christ his only Son our Lord, who was conceived by the Holy Ghost, born of the virgin Mary, suffered under Pontius Pilate, was crucified, dead, and buried: he descended into hell; the third day he rose again from the dead; he ascended into heaven, and sitteth on the right hand of God the Father Almighty; from thence he shall come to judge the quick and the dead. I believe in the Holy Ghost; the holy catholic church; the communion of saints; the forgiveness of sins; the resurrection of the body; and the life everlasting. Amen.

THE LORD'S PRAYER.

Our Father, which art in heaven, Hallowed be thy name. Thy kingdom come. Thy will be done on earth, as it is in heaven. Give us this day our daily bread, and forgive us our debts, as we forgive our debtors. And lead us not into temptation; but deliver us from evil: For thine is the kingdom, and the power, and the glory, for ever. Amen.

THE TEN COMMANDMENTS.

I. I am the Lord thy God, which have brought thee out of the land of Egypt, out of the house of bondage. Thou shalt have no other gods before me.

II. Thou shalt not make unto thee any graven image, or any likeness of any thing that is in heaven above, or that is in the earth beneath, or that is in the water under the earth: Thou shalt not bow down thyself to them, nor serve them: for I the Lord thy God am a jealous God, visiting the iniquity of the fathers upon the children unto the third and fourth generation of them that hate me; and shewing mercy unto thousands of them that love me, and keep my commandments.

III. Thou shalt not take the name of the Lord thy God in vain: for the Lord will not hold him guiltless that taketh his name in vain.

IV. Remember the Sabbath-day, to keep it holy. Six days shalt thou labour, and do all thy work: but the seventh day is the sabbath of the Lord thy God: in it thou shalt not do any work, thou, nor thy son, nor thy daughter, thy man-servant, nor thy maid-servant, nor thy cattle, nor thy stranger that is within thy gates: for in six days the Lord made heaven and earth, the sea, and all that in them is, and rested the seventh day: wherefore the Lord blessed the sabbath-day, and hallowed it.

V. Honour thy father and thy mother: that thy days may be long upon the Land which the Lord thy God giveth thee.

VI. Thou shalt not kill.

VII. Thou shalt not commit adultery.

VIII. Thou shalt not steal.

IX. Thou shalt not bear false witness against thy neighbour.

X. Thou shalt not covet thy neighbour's house, thou shalt not covet thy neighbour's wife, nor his man-servant, nor his maid-servant, nor his ox, nor his ass, nor any thing that is thy neighbour's.

Quest. 3. Where is the Christian Religion most fully opened and entirely contained?

Ans. In the Holy Scriptures, especially of the New Testament: where, by Christ and his Apostles and Evangelists, inspired by His Spirit, the history of Christ and His Apostles is sufficiently delivered, the promises and doctrines of faith are perfected, the covenant of grace more clearly opened and church-offices, worship and discipline established: on the understanding whereof the strongest Christians may increase while they live on earth. .

The explained Profession of the Christian Religion.

I. I believe that there is One God, an infinite Spirit of life, understanding and will: perfectly powerful, wise and good: the Father, the Word and the Spirit, the Creator, Governor and End of all things: our absolute Owner, our most just Ruler and our most gracious Benefactor and most amiable Lord.

II. I believe that man being made in the image of God, an embodied spirit of life, understanding and will, with holy suavity, wisdom and love, to know and love and serve his Creator here and for ever, did by wilful sinning fall from his God, his holiness and innocency, under the wrath of God, the condemnation of his Law, and the slavery of the flesh, the world and the devil. And that God so loved the world that He gave His only Son to be their Redeemer, who being God and one with the Father, took our nature and became man : being conceived of the Holy Ghost, born of the virgin Mary, called Jesus Christ, who was perfectly holy [and] sinless, fulfilling all righteousness, overcame the devil and the world and gave Himself a sacrifice for our sins, by suffering a cursed death on the cross, to ransom us and reconcile us unto God : and was buried and went among the dead : the third day He rose again, having conquered death. And He fully established the covenant of grace, that all that truly repent and believe shall have the love of the Father, the grace of the Son and the communion of the Holy Spirit; and if they love God and obey him sincerely to the death, they shall be glorified with him in heaven for ever; and the unbelievers, impenitent and ungodly shall go to everlasting punishment. And having commanded his Apostles to preach the Gospel to all the world and promised His Spirit, He ascended into heaven : where He is the glorified Head over all things to the Church and our prevailing Intercessor with the Father : who will there receive the departed souls of the justified : and at the end of this world will come again and rouse all the dead and will judge all according to their works and justly execute his Judgment.

III. I believe that God the Holy Spirit was given by the Father and the Son, to the prophets, apostles and evangelists, to be their infallible guide in preaching and recording the doctrine of salvation : and the witness of its certain truth, by his manifold Divine operations : and to question, illuminate and sanctify all the believers, that they may renounce the flesh, the world and the devil. And all that are thus sanctified are one holy and catholic Church of Christ and must live in holy communion and have the pardon of their sins and shall have everlasting life.

The *Covenant or Covenants.*—Believing in God the Father, Son and Holy Spirit, I do perfectly, absolutely and resolutely give up myself to Him, my Creator and reconciled God and Father, my Saviour and Sanctifier: and repenting of my sins I renounce the devil, the world and the sinful desires of the flesh : and denying myself and taking up my cross, I consent to follow Christ the captain of my salvation, in hope of His promised grace and glory.

A short Catechism for those that have learned the first.

Quest. 1. What do you believe concerning God?

Ans. There is one only God, an infinite Spirit of life, understanding and will, most perfectly powerful, wise and good : the Father, the Word and the Spirit: the Creator, Governor and End of all things : our absolute Owner, our most just Ruler, and our most gracious and most amiable Father.

Quest. 2. What believe you of the Creation, and the nature of man and the law which was given to him?

Ans. God created all the world : and made man in his own image, an embodied spirit of life, understanding and will, with holy liveliness, wisdom and love: to know and and love serve his Maker here and for ever : and gave him the inferior creatures for his use ; but forbad him to eat of the tree of knowledge upon pain of death.

Quest. 3. What believe you of man's fall into sin and misery?

Ans. Man being tempted by Satan, did by wilful sinning fall from his holiness, his innocency, and his happiness, under the justice of God, the condemnation of his Law, and the slavery of the flesh, the world and the devil ; whence sinful, guilty and miserable natures are propagated to all mankind: and no mere creature is able to deliver us.

Quest. 4. What believe you of man's Redemption by Jesus Christ?

Ans. God so loved the world that He gave His only Son to be their Saviour: Who being God and One with the Father, took our nature and became man: being conceived by the Holy Ghost, born of the virgin Mary and called Jesus Christ: Who was perfectly holy, without sin, fulfilling all righteousness: and overcame the devil and the world; and gave himself a sacrifice for our sins, by suffering a cursed death on the Cross to ransom us and reconcile us unto God: and was buried and went among the dead: the third day He rose again, having conquered death; and having sealed the New Covenant with His blood, He commanded His apostles and other ministers, to preach the Gospel to all the world: and promised the Holy Ghost: and then ascended into heaven, where He is God and man, the glorified Head over all things to His Church, and our prevailing intercessor with God the Father.

Quest. 5. What is the New Testament or Covenant or law of grace?

Ans. God through Jesus Christ doth freely give to all mankind Himself, to be their reconciled God and Father, the Son to be their Saviour, and the Holy Spirit to be their Sanctifier, if they will believe and accept the gift and will give up themselves to Him accordingly: repenting of their sins and consenting to forsake the devil, the world and the flesh, and sincerely, though not perfectly, to obey Christ and the Spirit to the end, according to the law of nature and the gospel institutions, that they may be glorified in heaven for ever.

Quest. 6. What believe ye of the Holy Ghost?

Ans. God the Holy Ghost was given by the Father and the Son to the prophets, apostles and evangelists, to be their infallible guide in preaching and recording the doctrine of salvation: and the witness of its certain truth by his manifold Divine operations. And He is given to quicken, illuminate and sanctify all true believers, and to save them from the devil, the world and the flesh.

Quest. 7. What believe you of the holy Catholic Church, the communion of saints and the forgiveness of sins?

Ans. All that truly consent to the baptismal covenant, are one sanctified Church or Body of Christ, and have communion in the same spirit of faith and love, and have the forgiveness of all their sins: and all that by baptism sensibly covenant and that continue to profess Christianity and holiness, are the universal visible Church or state: and must keep holy communion with love and peace in the particular Churches: in the doctrine, worship and order instituted by Christ.

Quest. 8. What believe you of the Resurrection and everlasting life?

Ans. At death the souls of the justified go to happiness with Christ, and the souls of the wicked to misery: and at the end of the world Christ will come in glory and will raise the bodies of all men from death and will judge all according to their works: and the righteous shall go into everlasting life where being made perfect themselves, they shall see God and perfectly love and praise Him, with Christ and all the glorified Church: and the rest into everlasting punishment.

Quest. 9. You have told me what you believe: Tell me now what is the full resolution and desire of your will concerning all this which you believe.

Ans. Believing in God the Father, Son and Holy Spirit, I do presently, absolutely and resolutely give up myself to Him, my Creator and reconciled God and Father, my Saviour and my Sanctifier! And repenting of my sins I renounce the devil, the world and the sinful desires of the flesh. And denying myself and taking up my cross, I consent to follow Christ, the captain of my Salvation: in hope of the grace and glory promised. Which I daily desire and beg as He hath taught me saying Our Father which art in heaven, etc.

Quest. 10. What is the practice which by this covenant you are obliged to?

Ans. According to the law of nature and Christ's institutions I must—desiring perfection—sincerely obey Him in a life of faith and hope and love: loving God as God for Himself above all, and loving myself as His servant, especially my soul, and seeking its holiness and salvation: and loving my neighbour as myself. I must avoid all idolatry of mind and body, and must worship God according to His Word, by learning and meditating on His Word: by prayer, thanksgiving, and praise and use of his Sacrament.*

I must not profane but holily use His holy name: I must keep holy the Lord's Day, especially in communion with the Church-assemblies: I must honour and obey my parents, magistrates, pastors and other rulers: I must not wrong my neighbour in thought, word or deed, in his soul, his body, his chastity, estate, right or propriety [=property]: but do him all the good I can: and do as I would be done by: which is summed up in the Ten Commandments 'God spake these words, saying,' etc.

A Prayer for Families in the method of the Lord's Prayer, being but an Exposition of it. Most glorious God, who art Power and Wisdom and Goodness itself, the Creator of all things: the Owner, the Ruler and the Benefactor of the world: though by sin, original and natural we were Thy enemies, the slaves of Satan and our flesh, and under Thy displeasure and the condemnation of Thy Law: yet Thy children redeemed by Jesus Christ Thy Son, and regenerated by Thy Holy Spirit, have leave to call Thee their reconciled Father. For by Thy covenant of grace Thou hast given them Thy Son to be their Head, their Teacher and their Saviour: and in Him Thou hast pardoned, adopted and sanctified them: sealing and preparing them for Thy

---

* The Lord's Supper and other Church-ordinances are referred to in the VIIIth day's Conference, and more fully in my 'Universal Concord.'—[See my List of Baxter's Writings. G.]

celestial kingdom and beginning in them that holy life and light and love which shall be perfected with Thee in everlasting Glory. O with what wondrous love hast Thou loved us, that of rebels we should be made the sons of God! Thou hast advanced us to this dignity that we might be elevated wholly to Thee as Thine own, and might delightfully obey Thee and actively love Thee with all our heart: and so might glorify Thee here and forever.

O cause both us and all Thy churches, and all the world, to hallow Thy great and holy name! and to live to Thee as our ultimate end : that Thy shining image and holy soul may glorify Thy divine perfection.

And cause both us and all the earth to cast off the tyranny of Satan and the flesh and to acknowledge Thy supreme authority and to become the kingdoms of Thee and Thy Son Jesus, by a willing and absolute subjection. O perfect Thy kingdom of grace in ourselves and in the world and hasten the kingdom of glory.

And cause us and thy churches and all people of the earth no more to be ruled by the lusts of the flesh and their erroneous conceits, and by self-will, which is the idol of the wicked : but by Thy perfect wisdom and holy will revealed in Thy laws. Make known Thy Word to all the world and send them the messengers of grace and peace : and cause men to understand, believe and obey the Gospel of salvation, and that with such holiness, unity and love, that the Earth which is now too like hell may be made liker unto heaven : and not only Thy scattered, imperfect flock but those also who in their carnal and ungodly minds do now refuse a holy life and think Thy word and ways too strict, may desire to imitate even the heavenly Church: where Thou art obeyed and loved and praised, with high delight, in harmony and perfection :

And because our being is the subject of our well-being, maintain us in the life which Thou hast here given us, until the work of life be finished : and give us such health of mind and body and such protection and supply of all our wants as shall fit us for our duty and make us contented with our daily bread and patient if we want it. And save us from the love of the riches and honours and pleasures of this world; and the pride, and idleness and sensuality which they cherish. And cause us to serve Thy Providence by our diligent labours, and to serve Thee faithfully with all that Thou givest us. And let us not make provision for the flesh to satisfy its desires and lusts.

And we beseech Thee of Thy mercy, through the sacrifice and propitiation of Thy beloved Son, forgive us all our sins, original and actual, from our birth to this hour : our omissions of duty and committing what Thou didst forbid : our sins of heart and word and deed; our sinful thoughts and affections, our sinful passions and discontents, our secret and our open sins, our sins of negligence and ignorance and rashness : but especially our sins against knowledge and conscience, which have made the deepest guilt and wounds. Spare us O Lord and let not our sins so find us out as to be our ruin : but let us so find them out as truly to repent and turn to Thee! Especially punish us not with the loss of Thy grace! Take not Thy Holy Spirit from us and deny us not Thy assistance and holy operations. Seal to us by that Spirit the pardon of our sins, and lift up the light of Thy countenance upon us and give us the joy of Thy favour and salvation. And let thy love and mercy so fill us not only with thankfulness to Thee : but with love and mercy to our brethren and our enemies, that we may heartily forgive them that do us wrong, as through Thy grace we hope we do. And for the time to come, suffer us not to cast ourselves wilfully into temptations : but carefully to avoid them and resolutely to resist and conquer what we cannot avoid. And O sanctify those inward sins and lusts which are our constant and most dangerous temptations : and let us not be tempted by Satan or the world, or tried by Thy judgments above the strength which Thy grace shall give us. Save us from a fearless confidence in our own strength. And let us not dally with the snare nor taste the bait nor play with the fire of Thy wrath: but cause us to fear and depart from evil: lest before we are aware we be entangled and overcome and wounded with our guilt and with Thy wrath, and our end should be worse than our beginning. Especially save us from those radical sins of error and unbelief, pride, hypocrisy, hardheartedness, sensuality, slothfulness and the love of the present world and the loss of our love to Thee, to Thy kingdom and Thy ways.

And save us from the malice of Satan and of wicked men and from the evils which our sins would bring upon us.

And as we crave all this from Thee, we humbly render our praises with our future service to Thee! Thou art the king of all the world and more than the life of all the living! Thy kingdom is everlasting! Wise and just and merciful is Thy government. Blessed are they that are Thy faithful subjects. But who hath hardened himself against Thee and hath prospered? The whole creation proclaimeth Thy perfection: But it is to heaven where the blessed see Thy glory and the glory of our Redeemer, where the angels and saints behold Thee, admire Thee, adore Thee, love Thee, and praise Thee with triumphant, joyful songs, the holy, holy, holy God, the Father, Son and Holy Ghost, who was and is and is to come. Of Thee and through Thee and to Thee are all things. To Thee be glory for ever. Amen.

A Short Prayer for Families.

Most glorious, ever-living God, Father, Son and Holy Ghost, infinite in Thy power, wisdom and goodness! Thou art the Author of all the world, the Redeemer of lost mankind, and the Sanctifier of Thine elect! Thou hast made us living, reasonable souls, placed awhile on earth in flesh, to seek and know and love and serve Thee, which we should have done with all our soul and might. For we and all things are Thine own and Thou art more to us than all the world. This should have been the greatest business care and pleasure of our lives. We were bound to it by Thy Law and invited by Thy love and mercy and the promise of a reward in heaven. And in our baptism we were devoted to this Christian life of faith and holiness, by a solemn covenant and vow. But with grief and shame we do confess that we have been too unfaithful to that covenant and too much neglected the Lord our Father, our Saviour and our Sanctifier, to whom we were devoted. And have too much served the flesh and the world and the devil which we renounced. We have added to our original sin, the guilt of unthankfulness for a Saviour and resisting the Spirit and grace that should have renewed, governed and saved us. We have spent much of our lives in fleshly and worldly vanity and wilfully neglected the greatest work of making a sure preparation for death and judgment and our endless state. In a custom of sinning we have hardened our hearts against Thy Word and warnings and the reproofs of thy ministers and of our consciences that have oft told us of our sin and danger and called us to repent. And now O Lord! our convinced souls confess that we deserve to be forsaken by Thee and left to our own lust and folly and to the deceits of Satan and unto endless misery. But seeing Thou hast given a Saviour to lost man and a pardoning covenant through the merits of Christ, promising forgiveness and salvation to every true, penitent, believer, we thankfully accept Thy offered mercy and penitently bewail our sin and cast our miserable souls upon Thy grace and the sacrifice, merits and intercession of our Redeemer.

Forgive all the sins of our hearts and lives; and as a reconciled Father take us as Thy adopted children in

Christ. O give us Thy renewing Spirit to be in us a powerful and constant author of holy light and love and life, to fit us for all our duty and for communion with Thee and for everlasting life. And to dwell in us as Thy witness and seal of our adoption. Let Him be better to our souls than our souls are to our bodies, teaching us Thy word and will, and bringing all our love and will to a joyful compliance with Thy will and quickening our dull and drowsy hearts to a holy and heavenly conversation. Let Him turn all our sinful pleasures and desires unto the delightful love of Thee and of Thy ways and servants. Save us from the great sins of selfishness pride and worldliness, and give us self-denial, humility and a heavenly mind, that while we are on earth, our hearts may be in heaven, where we hope to live in Thy joyful love and praise, with Christ and all His holy ones for ever. Let us never forget that this life is short and that the life to come is endless: that our souls are precious and our bodies vile and must shortly turn to rottenness and dust: that sin is odious and temptation dangerous and judgment dreadful to unprepared, guilty souls: and that to them a Saviour and His grace and Spirit there is no salvation. Cause us to live as we would die, and let no temptation, company or business, draw us to forget our God and our everlasting state.

Lord bless the world, and specially these kingdoms, with wise, godly, just and peaceable princes and inferior judges and magistrates; and guide, protect and perfect them for the common good and the promoting of godliness and suppressing of sin. And bless all Churches with able, godly, faithful Pastors, that are zealous lovers of God and goodness and the people's souls. And save the nations and churches from oppressing tyrants and deceivers, and from malignant enemies to serious piety. And cause subjects to live in just obedience and in love and peace. Bless Families with wise, religious governors, who will carefully instruct their children and servants and restrain them from sin and keep them from temptation. Teach children and servants to fear God and honour and obey their governors.

O our Father which art in heaven, let Thy name be hallowed: Let Thy kingdom come: Let Thy will be done on earth as it is in heaven: Give us this day our daily bread: Forgive us our trespasses as we forgive them that trespass against us: Lead us not into temptation but deliver us from evil: for Thine is the kingdom, the power and the glory for ever. Amen.

Before Meat.

Most gracious God, who hast given us Christ and with Him all that is necessary to life and godliness: we thankfully take this our food as the gift of Thy bounty, procured by His merits. Bless it to the nourishment and strength of our frail bodies to fit us for Thy cheerful service. And save us from the abuse of Thy mercies by gluttony, drunkenness, idleness and sinful fleshly lusts, for the sake of Jesus Christ our only Saviour and Lord. Amen.

After Meat.

Most merciful Father, accept of our thanks for these and all Thy mercies: and give us yet more thankful hearts. O give us more of the great mercies proper to Thy children, even Thy sanctifying and comforting Spirit, assurance of Thy love through Christ and a treasure and a heart and conversation in heaven. And bring and keep us in a constant readiness for a safe and comfortable death: for the sake of Jesus Christ our Lord and only Saviour. Amen.

FINIS.

D

Annotated List

OF THE

WRITINGS

- OF

RICHARD BAXTER

•

AUTHOR OF

The Saint's Everlasting Rest

Made from

COPIES

OF

THE BOOKS AND TRACTATES

THEMSELVES

BY

THE REV. ALEXANDER B. GROSART,

LIVERPOOL.

'How true time is to the real character of the men whose wrongs it avenges, and whose merits it rewards! The proverbial epithet "The holy Baxter" (like that older one "The venerable Bede"), is just the verdict which a seraph "full of eyes within and without," might be expected to pronounce after having deliberately reviewed the whole history and works of the sage of Kidderminster."

HENRY ROGERS, author of 'The Eclipse of Faith,' etc. etc.

PRINTED FOR PRIVATE CIRCULATION.

1868.

PREFATORY NOTE.

I HOPE to be able to complete in a goodly number of years hence a '*labour of love*' on which I have been long occupied viz., a full and accurate enumeration of the Writings of the Puritans, earlier and later, and of the 'Ejected' of 1662—from a personal examination of their books and tractates themselves, *not* from Catalogues or other compilations. This, preparatory to an Introduction to the Theological Literature of our Country.

I offer meanwhile the present 'Annotated List' of the numerous Works of RICHARD BAXTER as a specimen of the Catalogue I propose to draw up. I venture to believe that it will be found accurate, and much more extensive than any extant. With the trifling exceptions noted in their places it has been my rare good fortune to have had access to the entire Writings of our Worthy in the original and early editions. Nearly all indeed, are contained in my own Library. In the Catalogue above promised ('if the Lord will') I intend adding (*a*) Those books to which BAXTER prefixed 'Preface' or 'Epistle' (*b*) *Manuscripts* in Williams' Library and elsewhere—(*c*) Translations of his Writings (*d*) Books and tractates in controversy, or otherwise relating to him. (*a*) Will bring up the List to (it is believed) 200 distinct publications: and I may observe that many of his 'Prefaces' and 'Epistles' are really priceless 'Essays' and even treatises on the subject of which they treat.*

This is not the place to enter on an examination of the *characteristics* of the Writings recorded in this List. The great Dr ISAAC BARROW long ago said of them—" His *practical* writings were never mended, and his *controversial* ones seldom confuted" [Calamy 'Account' vol. i. p. 422]: Bishop Wilkins observed, " He cultivated every subject he handled, and if he had lived in the primitive times he had been one of the Fathers of the Church. It is enough for one age to produce such a person as Richard Baxter' ['Gift of Preaching']; and, stout Churchman though he was,—DR SAMUEL JOHNSON, when he was asked by BOSWELL what works of Baxter he should read, said, " Read any of them: they are all good' ['Life' c. lxxvi]: and again and again shewed that he had himself read them. He deemed it a sufficient reason for resolving to study a treatise of GROTIUS that Baxter had recommended it. [See 'Life' under BAXTER, for various references].

* There have been many exaggerations of the extent of BAXTER's Works : but the most astounding is the following from Drs M'Clintock's and Strong's "Cyclopædia of Biblical, Theological, and Ecclesiastical Literature. Vol. I. A B. New York 1867 *sub nomine* " In all he is said to have composed one hundred and forty-five works in *folio* and sixty-three in *quarto*, besides a multitude of more trifling writings!' A number of treatises in Latin are named that have no existence : the explanation being that the writer of the 'notice' was copying from some continental bibliographic work wherein the English titles are rendered into Latin, as Walch does.—All the Lists of Baxter and of our Theology that I have met with commit like blunders from their *second-hand* character. This renders Watt's Bibliotheca, Allibone *et hoc genus omne* unreliable.—ORME's List at close of his 'Life' of Baxter (Vol. I. of the 'Practical Works,' 23 vols. 8vo. 1830) extends to 168: and it is one of many illustrations of the worthlessness of any such enumeration taken at second-hand. It not only splits up one work into several, but so misdivides others as to show that he had never seen the books or tractates, relying on Calamy and Catalogues. The same remark, somewhat modified, applies to the list in Darling's 'Cyclopædia Bibliographica,' etc. etc.

Prefatory Note.

I close this 'Note' with Baxter's own 'censure' (Calamy's word) of his Writings, which, to my mind, is very beautiful in its humility: "concerning almost all my Writings, I must confess that my own judgment is that fewer well studied and polished would have been better: but the reader who can safely censure the books is not fit to censure the Author, unless he had been upon the place and acquainted with all the occasions and circumstances. Indeed, for the *Saint's Rest* I had four months vacancy to write it (but in the midst of continual languishing and medicine). But for the rest I wrote them in the crowd of my other employments which would allow me no great leisure for polishing and exactness or any ornament: so that I scarce ever wrote one sheet twice over nor stayed to make any blots or interlinings, but was fain to let it go as it was first conceived. And when my own desire was rather to stay upon one thing long than run over many, some sudden occasions or other, extorted almost all my writings from me: and the apprehensions of present usefulness or necessity, prevailed against all other motives. So that the Divines which were at hand with me still put me on and approved of what I did, because they were moved by present necessities as well as I: but those that were far off and felt not these nearer motives, did rather wish that I had taken the other way and published a few elaborate writings: and I was ready myself to be of their mind when I forgot the case that then I stood in and have lost the sense of former motives. The opposing of the Anabaptists, Separatists, Quakers, Antinomians, Seekers, etc., were works which *then* seemed necessary: and so did the debates about the church-government and communion, which touched our present practice. But now all those reasons are past and gone I could wish I had rather been doing some work of more durable usefulness. But even to a foreseeing man who knoweth what will be of longest use, it is hard to discern how far that which is presently useful may be omitted for the sake of a greater future good. There are some other works wherein my heart hath more been set than any of these fore-mentioned: in which I have met with great obstructions. For I must declare that in this as among other matters I have found that we are not the choosers of our own employments, no more than of our own successes.' [Reliquiæ Lib. i. page 124]— Curiously enough the most imperfect and inaccurate list of BAXTER'S Writings is his own in the 'Reliquiæ.' He forgot many, and ante-dates and post-dates, and otherwise mis-describes.

It will much oblige me if any one who chances to see this booklet will kindly inform me where I can find the few in this List uncollated: and also any of the earlier (contemporary) translations into German, Dutch, French, etc. I shall cordially acknowledge help rendered.

ALEXANDER B. GROSART.

Liverpool.

ANNOTATED LIST OF BAXTER'S WRITINGS.

I. APHORISMES of JUSTIFICATION, with their Explication annexed. Wherein also is opened the nature of the Covenants, Satisfaction, Righteousnesse, Faith, Works, &c. Published especially for the use of the Church of Kederminster in Worcestershire. By their unworthy Teacher RI. BAXTER. Hebr. 9. 15. London, Printed for Francis Tyton, at the Three Daggers in Fleet Street, neer the Inner - Temple Gate. 1649 [18mo].

Collation: Title-page — the Epistle Dedicatory 'To the learned, zealous, faithfull ministers of Jesus Christ, Mr Richard Vines, Master of Pembroke-Hall in Cambridge and Mr Anthony Burges, Pastor of Sutton-Coldfield in Warwickshire, members of the Reverend Assembly of Divines, my very much valued friends and brethren in the work and patience of the Gospel' pp. 10—to the Reader pp. 21—treatise pp. 335—'the chief-distinctions upon which this discourse dependeth' pp. 11 — postscript 1 page.

The 'Aphorisms' appears to have been submitted to some friend in manuscript; for in complete copies of the book there is found the following:—

'An Appendix to the foregoing Treatise being an answer to the Objections of a Friend concerning some points therein contained, and at his own desire annexed for the sake of others that may have the same thoughts,' pp. 188.

In the '*Reliquiæ Baxterianæ*' [No. cliv.] Baxter gives a characteristic account of the origin and reception of the 'Aphorisms.' He recognizes with rare candour the ability and worth of those who wrote against his book. See Part I. pp. 107-108 ; and cf. Calamy's Abridgement Vol. I. pp. 410-411. My friend Joshua Wilson Esq. of Tunbridge Wells, has an edition of the 'Aphorisms' [1655 24mo] bearing the imprint of 'the Hague:' but which was actually printed at Cambridge: See Baxter's 'Catholic Theology,' Preface p. v.: also Answer to Dr Tullie's Letter,' p. 10 on this surreptitious edition.

Mr Wilson's copy formerly belonged to the Author himself. There are some MS. corrections by him and some critical remarks on a fly-leaf before the title-page, concluding thus 'All which I have fully open'd in many books written long after this upon riper thoughts: this being the first that ever I wrote in my immature youth, in the crudity of my new conceptions. Cf. Orme's Life and Times of Baxter, II. 38. In the 'Postscript' (above noted) reference is made to an intended publication 'Universal Redemption' [No. CLIV.] but which he postponed because of 'continued sickness' and as also 'observing how many lately are set a-work on the same subject, as Whitfield, Stalham, Howe, Owen, and some men of note now upon it.' In a short address to the Reader prefixed to the 'Appendix' we have this apology. 'The disorder of the interrogations and objections which extorted from me this whole tractate by pieces one after another, hath caused me—an unfeigned lover of method—to give thee such a disorderly, unmethodical miscellany;' and again, after explanations 'These things need no excuse but this information: That I was to follow and not to lead, and that I wrote only for those who knew less than myself. If thou know more, thank God and join with me for the instruction of the ignorant, whose information, reformation and salvation, and thereby God's glory is the top of my ambition.' For notices of VINES and BURGES (or Burgess) to whom the 'Aphorisms' is dedicated, see Brook's 'Lives of the Puritans' for the former [Vol. III. pp. 230-235], and for the latter Calamy '*Account*' [Vol. II. pp. 739-740 and page 853 '*Continuation*.']

II. THE SAINT'S EVERLASTING REST: or a Treatise of the blessed state of the Saints in their enjoyment of God in Glory. Wherein is shewed its excellency and certainty; the misery of those that lose it, the way to attain it and assurance of it; and how to live in the continual delightful foretasts of it by the help of meditation. Written by the Author for his own use in the time of his languishing, when God took him off from all publike imployment; and afterwards preached in his weekly Lecture: and now published by Richard Baxter, Teacher of the Church of Kederminster in Worestershire. London, Printed by Rob. White for Thomas Underhil and Francis Tyton, and are to be sold at the Blue Anchor and Bible in Pauls Church-yard, near the little North-door, and at the three Daggers in Fleetstreet, near the Inner-Temple gate. 1650 [4°.]

(1) 1st. edn. 1650. *Collation*: Title-page [on which is the 'License' thus 'Jan. 15, 1649. Imprimatur, Joseph Caryl' the 'Licenser' being the erudite and venerable Commentator on 'Job']— Epistle Dedicatory of 'the whole' book to 'my dearly beloved friends, the inhabitants of the Burrough and Sovereign of Kederminster, both magistrates and people' pp. 11—Epistle Dedicatory of 'the First Part' to 'the right Worshipful Sir Thomas Rous, Baronet, with the Lady Jane Rous, his wife' pp. 3—Contents or Table pp. 8—Treatise as follows:

1st Part pp. 164—On page 164 'Finis'—Next a separate title 'The Saint's Everlasting Rest. The Second Part. Containing the Proofes of the Truth and certain futurity of our Rest. And that the Scripture promising that Rest to us is the perfect infallible Word and Law of God. London, Printed by Rob. White for T. Underhill and F. Tyton, and are to be sold at the sign of the Bible in great Woodstreet and at the three daggers in Fleet-street, 1649.

Then, Epistle Dedicatory 'To my dearly beloved Friends the inhabitants of Bridgnorth, both magistrates and people. Richard Baxter devoteth this part of this Treatise. In testimony of his unfeigned love to them who were the first to whom he was sent (or fixed) to publish the Gospel. And in thankfulness to the Divine Majesty who there priviledged and protected him' pp. 2—To the Reader pp. 8, dated 'Jan. 18, 1649—Part II. pp. 167-260. Next, a separate title The Saint's Everlasting Rest. The Third Part. Containing severall Uses of the former Doctrine of Rest. London [as before]. Then, Epistle Dedicatory 'To my dearly beloved Friends the inhabitants of the city of Coventry both magistrates and people: especially Col. John Barker and Col. Tho. Willoughby, late Governors, with all the officers and soldiers of their garrison. Rich. Baxter devoteth this Part of this Treatise in thankful acknowledgment of their great affection toward him and ready acceptance of his labors among them — which is the highest recompense, if joyned with obedience, that a faithful minister can expect, pp. 2.—Part III. pp. 263-551. Next a separate title 'The Saint's Everlasting Rest. The Fourth Part. Containing a Directory for the getting and keeping of the heart in heaven: by the diligent practice of that excellent unknown duty of Heavenly Meditation. Being the main thing intended by the Author in the writing of this book: and to which all the rest is but subservient. London [as before]. Then, Epistle Dedicatory 'To my dearly beloved friends in the Lord, the inhabitants of the town of Shrewsbury, both magistrates, ministers, and people, as also of the neighbouring parts. Rich. Baxter devoteth this practicale part of this Treatise as a testimony of his love to his native soyl and to his many godly and faithfull friends there living' pp. 2—The Introduction pp. 555-558—Pt. IV. pp. 559-848—On fly-leaf, first side 'Errata,' headed 'If you will reade nothing but what was intended by the Author amend these misprintings: the rest are but small.'

(2) 2*d edn.* 1651. Same title-page except 'The second edition corrected and enlarged,' and 'Underhill' spelled so and not with a single l as in 1st edn.

Collation: Title-page—Ep: Dedy. pp. 13—to Rous pp. 3—A Premonition 'as to alterations and additions' pp. 12 dated 'May 17, 1651'; a singularly interesting autobiographic Address—Contents pp. 8 'Errata' on the last page— Pt. I. pp. 184—separate title—as before —London [as in general title, *supra*]— Ep: Dedy. pp. 2—the Preface pp. 35 valuable and searching—Pt. II. pp. 185-304.

Separate title [as before]—Ep. Dedy pp. 2—Pt. III. pp., 312 [separate pagination] 'Finis' on page 312—Separate title—[as before]— Ep. Dedy. 1 page—'the Introduction pp. 4-6—Pt. IV. pp. 7-304 [also separate pagination'].

(3) 3*d edn*: 1652—Title-page as before except 'The third edition' and at bottom 'by Rob. White' left out.

Collation: Title-page. Ep: Dedy pp. 13—to Rous pp. 3. Premonition [which still reads as for 'second' edn.] pp. 12. Contents pp. 8. Pt. I. pp. 184. Separate title. Ep: Dedy. pp. 2. Preface pp. 35. Pt. II. pp. 185-304. Separte title. Ep: Dedy pp. 2. Pt. III. pp. 368 [separate pagn.] Separate title. Ep.: Dedy. 1 page. Introdn. pp. 4-6. Pt. IV. pp. 7-304. Then 'Broughton in the conclusion of his concent of Scripture' pp. 305-308. Herbert's poem of 'Home' pp. 309-311. Questions discussed 1 page. Alphabetical Table pp. 4.

⁕⁕ 'Finis on page 304: and what follows after awanting.

(4) 4*th edn.* 1653. Title-page as before except 'The fourth edition.'

Collation: Title-page. Ep. Dedy. pp. 13—to Rous pp. 3. Premonition [still as before] pp. 12. Contents pp. 8. Pt. I. pp. 183.

At page 160 follows in this edition two and a half pages unpaged confessing a mistake in 'doctrine'(very curious). Then goes on from the last of these pages, and so pp. 161 to 183 as *supra*—which explains the mispaging of 183 instead of 184. Separate title. Ep. Dedy. on reverse. Preface pp. 35. Pt. II. 185-304. Separate title. Ep. Dy. pp. 2. Pt. III. pp. 368 'Finis' on page 368 [as before]. Separate title. Ep. Dy. on page 3. Intro. pp. 4-6. Pt. IV. pp. 7-304: and as in 3d edn. follg.

(5) 5*th edn.* 1654. Title-page as before except 'The fifth edition.' All as before but after the final Table 'An Addition to the 11th chapter of the 3d Part' pp. 8.

(6) 6*th edn.* 1656. Title-page as before except 'The sixth edn.' All exactly as before in 5th edn.

⁕⁕ In Abp. Marsh's 'Library' Dublin, the copy of this edition has the autograph of Mich. Jephson and th Greek motto πανταχῇ τ]ιν ἀλήθειαν

(7) 7*th edn.* 1658. Title-page same as before except 'The seventh edition revised by the Author.' Prefixed is a curious emblematical engraved title.

Collation: Title-page *as supra*. Ep. Dy. pp. 11—to Rous pp. 2. Premonition pp. 7 [as before] Contents pp. 5. Pt. I. pp. 153. Separate title. Ep. Dy. pp. 2. Preface pp. 159-187. Pt. II. pp. 189-291. Separate title. Ep. Dy. pp. 2. Pt. III. pp. 297-580. Separate title. Ep. Dy. pp. 2. Intro. pp. 2. Pt. III. 587-815. Then as before pp. 817-829. But then pp.

830-836 dated 'Jan. 15, 1657' to the Reader added. Table pp. 3.

(8) *8th edn.* 1659. Title-pages as in 7th : except 'the eighth edition.' All the rest the same as 7th.

(9) *9th edn.* I have not happened to meet with this.

(10) *10th edn.* 1669. Title-pages as before, except 'the tenth edition.' All the rest the same—but publisher as follows 'London Printed by R. W. for Francis Tyton and are to be sold at the sign of the three daggers in Fleet Street.'

(11) *11th edn.* 1671 and also one so designated 1677. Title-pages as before, except 'the eleventh edition'—and added to publisher as follows 'And Robert Boulter at the Turk's Head over against the Royal Exchange in Cornhil.' All the rest the same.

₊ Portrait is sometimes inserted 'ætat 55, 1670.'

(12) *12th edn.* 1688. Same book in all respects but pp. 796 instead of pp. 836 as *supra*. ☞ I note that after the 'Restoration' the famous passage in which the Patriots of the Commonwealth are named as in glory, is omitted. Cf page 86 of 1st edition : page 101 of 2d, ditto of 3d to 6th, page 83 of 7th and 8th : left out in 10th page 83—Such names were not to be exposed to the contumely of a degenerate succeeding generation.

₊ It will interest the Reader to have Baxter's own account of this imperishable book from the ' Reliquiæ :'—'The second book which I wrote — and the first which I began — was that called ' The Saint's Everlasting Rest :' Whilst I was in health I had not the least thought of writing books or of serving God in any more public' way than preaching. But when I was weakened with great bleeding and left solitary in my chamber at Sir John Cook's [Coke's ?] in Derbyshire without any acquaintance but my servant about me, and was sentenced to death by the physicians, I began to contemplate more seriously on the Everlasting Rest which I apprehended myself to be just on the borders of. And that my thoughts might not too much scatter in my meditation I began to write something on that subject, intending but the quantity of a sermon or two—which is the cause that the beginning is in brevity and style disproportionable to the rest : but being continued long in weakness where I had no books nor no better employment I followed it on till it was enlarged to the bulk in which it was published. The first three weeks I spent on it was at Mr Nowel's house at Kirby-Mallory in Leicestershire ; a quarter of a year more at the seasons which so great weakness would allow, I bestowed on it at Sir Thomas Rous's house at Rous-Lench in Worcestershire ; and I finished it shortly after at Kidderminster. The first and last parts were first done, being all that I intended for my own use : and the second and third parts came afterwards in besides my own intention. This Book it pleased God so far to bless to the profit of many that it encouraged me to be guilty of all those scripts which after followed. The marginal citations I put in after I came home to my books ; but almost all the book itself was written when I had no book but a Bible and a Concordance ; and I found that the transcript of the heart hath the greatest force on the hearts of others. For the good that I have heard that multitudes received by that writing and the benefits which I have again received by their prayers I here humbly return my thanks to Him that compelled me to write it." [*As before* Part I. page 108.] To this it were a pleasant but here an impossible task to cull the many tributes paid to this holy and hallowing book by the foremost men of this generation : and equally so to record actual cases of highest good done by it in all ranks and languages. Of the latter I would remind of the conversion thereby of Janeway [See his "Life"] : and may mention a very interesting fact, viz., that in Apsley House, shortly after the death of the Duke of Wellington I was shewn a copy of ' The Saint's Everlasting Rest ' [Fawcett's abridged edition] with a corner of a leaf turned down to mark the place where the great Soldier had "left off" on departing for Walmer Castle. *It is the last book his Grace is known to have read :* and that within a few days of "the end." It is fine to think of " the old grey head" bent over the old Puritan's heaven-disclosing book.

III. Plain Scripture Proof of Infants Church-membership and Baptism : being the Arguments prepared for (and partly managed) in the publike Dispute with Mr Tombes at Bewdley on the first day of January 1649. With a full Reply to what he then answered and what is contained in his Sermon since preached, in his printed Books, his MS. on 1 Cor. 7. 14 which I saw, against Mr Marshall against these arguments. With a Reply to his valedictory oration at Bewdley and a Corrective for his Antidote. By Richard Baxter, a Minister of Christ for his Church at Kederminster. Constrained unavoidably hereto by Mr Tombes, his importunity : by frequent Letters, Messengers, in his Pulpit, and at last in print, calling out for my arguments and charging the denial upon my conscience. Hereto is added an Appendix against the Doctrine in the other extream contained in a tractate of Mr Th. Bedford's adorned with the great names and pretended concent of famous learned Dr Davenant and Dr Usher ; and with an Epistle of Mr Cranford's, and a tractate of Dr Ward's (on which also some Animadversions are added.) London, printed for Robert White 1651. [Sm. 4°.]

Collation: Title-page—two leaves of quotations from Scripture, the Fathers, etc. Epistle Dedicatory in double columns headed respectively 'To the Church at Kederminster, my dearly beloved, my crown and my joy' and 'To the Church at Bewdley, my unfaignedly beloved friends in the Lord' pp. 11. "The true History of the Conception and Nativity of this treatise ; being the author's Apology for his attempt of this unpleasant task' pp. 25. The Contents, with Errata, on last page pp. 10. Treatise pp. 1–286.

After page 162 a separate title 'An Answer to Mr Tombes his valedictory oration to the people of Berdley : in Vindication of the fifth Direction which I give my hearers of Kederminster in the Preface of my book, entituled 'The Saint's Everlasting Rest' with a brief confutation of six more of Mr T.'s errors and a Correction for his Antidote and Confutation-Sermon. Being the third part of this treatise. Extorted unavoidably from one that abhorreth division and contention and bendeth his prayers and studies for the peace of the Church. London, printed Anno Dom. 1651 After page 233 another separate title 'A Corrective for a circumforaneous Antidote against the verity of a passage in the Epistle before my treatise of Rest. London [as before.]

After page 286 there is a separate title-page as follows, 'An Appendix being some brief Animadversions on a Tractate lately published by Mr Th. Bedford ; and honored with the great names and pretended consent of famous, learned, judicious Davenant and Usher, with an Epistle of Mr Cranford, and a tractate of Dr Ward (on which also some Animadversions are added). Also an Addition to the fifteenth argument, chap. 20. of the first part of this book concerning the Universal Visible Church, occasioned by Mr Sam : Hudson's most judicious Vindication. And some Arguments against the old and new Socinians, who deny the continued use of Baptism to settled Churches, occasioned by the late eruption of that error. London, Printed Anno Dom. 1651.' A Premonition to the Reader pp. 289–290. Quotations pp. 291–292. Treatise pp. 293-343. The conclusion of this treatise page 344. Postscript 346.

See *'Reliquiæ'* for remarks by Baxter on the 'Plain Scripture Proof' and certain opinions concerning the 'salvation' of children. [As before, Pt. I. p. 109] A 'Postscript' to 'Plain Scripture Proof' (pp. 345, 346) contains a curious 'intimation' concerning the 'Aphorisms' [See No. I.] and asks that before a 'second edition' be published all who love the truth will send the Author their 'Animadversions' that he may himself profit and good otherwise be done.

See the *'Reliquiæ'* also for the circumstances out of which this book sprang and various interesting details concerning its influence : and for an explicit statement of Baxter's opinion on Infant-salvation as distinguished from Infant-baptism (merely)—☞ ORME gives the 'Animadversions' on Bedford and 'Letters' to and from Tombes, etc., as distinct works, one of many mistakes whereby he over-extends his List of Baxter's Writings and betrays not having seen the books themselves.

⁎ The 'fourth edition' of 'Plain Scripture Proof' 1656 (4°) 'printed for T. U. F. T. and are to be sold by John Wright at the King's Head in the Old Bailey' has considerable additions e.g. after page 346. 'A Friendly Accommodation in the fore-debated Controversie between Mr Bedford and the Author: wherein is manifested that the Differences are few and small; and those continued with mutual respect and love. London, Printed Anno Dom. 1656. On reverse of title a 'Note to Reader'—pp. 347–367. Then another: 'Præfestinantis Morator' or Mr Tombes his Precursor staid and examined, and proved not to be from heaven but of man. Yet God by Mr T. sendeth thus truth to the hearts of all whom it may concern Procurs. page 82, 83 [Pastors and Teachers or Presbyters to teach and govern the Church of God I am assured are a Divine institution and a very merciful gift of Christ, Ephesians iv. 11, 12, 13: 1 Corinthians xii. 28: Acts xiv. 23: 1 Timothy iii. 1: Titus ii. 5 to whom people should yield obedience Hebrews xiii. 7, 17 and yield maintenance liberally 1 Corinthians ix. 14: Galatians vi. 6: 1 Timothy v. 17, 18. If any go about to extirpate them, let him be accursed as an enemy to Christ and his Church.] Or if Socinus be of more authority with them let them receive the same truth from their Cracovian Catech. de Eccles. cap. 2. London, Printed in the year 1656. Contents pp. 371–372. Treatise pp. 373–401. Then 'Letters that passed between Mr Baxter and Mr Tombes concerning the Dispute. London Printed in the year 1656. On reverse of title a 'Note' on the publication. Letters pp. 405–415.

IV. The Right Method for a settled Peace of Conscience and Spiritual Comfort. In 32 Directions. Written for the use of a troubled friend: and now published by Richard Baxter, Teacher of the Church at Kederminster in Worcestershire. London, Printed for T. Underhill, F. Tyton and W. Raybould, and are to be sold at the Anchor and at the Unicorn in Pauls Church-yard, and at the Three Daggers in Fleetstreet 1653 [12°.]

Collation: 1 Leaf of texts of Scripture and at the end 'Sound doctrine makes a sound judgment, a sound heart, a sound conversation, and a sound conscience'— Epistle Dedicatory 'to my much valued, beloved and honored friends Col. John Bridges, with Mrs Margaret Bridges his wife, and Mr Thomas Foley with Mrs Anne Foley, his wife," pp. 12—To the poor in spirit, pp. 23—The contents pp. 15—Errata 1 page—Treatise pp. 540.

In the '*Reliquiæ*' is given an account of the origin of this searching and still potential book—[As before Pt. I. pp. 109–110]—Baxter mentions that it had 'pleased much, Dr Hammond:' but adds 'the women and weaker sort I found could not so well improve clear reason as they can a few comfortable, warm and pretty sentences; it is style and not reason which doth most with them. And some of the Divines were angry with it for a passage or two about Perseverance, because I had said that many men are certain of their present sanctification which are not certain of their perseverance and salvation: meaning all the godly that are assured of their sanctification and yet do not hold the certainty of perseverance. But a great storm of jealousie and censure was by this and some such words raised against me, by many good men, who lay more on their opinions and party than they ought. Therefore whereas some would have had me to retract it and others to leave it out of the next impression, I did the latter, but instead of it I published not long after my book called "R. B.'s Judgment about the Perseverance of Believers." [*Infra.*]

⁎ In the same year "the second edition, corrected and augmented " the augmentation consisting of "An Apologie " at the end (pp. 19) explanatory of certain portions.

V. Christian Concord: or the Agreement of the Associated Pastors and Churches of Worcestershire. With Rich. Baxter's Explication and Defence of it and his Exhortation to Unity. London Printed by A. M. for Thomas Underhill, at the Anchor and Bible in Pauls Church-yard near the little north-door, and Francis Tyton at the three Daggers in Fleet-street near Dunstans Church. 1653 [4°].

Collation: Title-page — Passages of Scripture pp. 2—Propositions agreed on pp. 13—the Profession of the Associated Churches pp. 6—A separate title as follows :—'An Explication of some Passages in the foregoing Proposition and Profession, with an answer to some Objections that are like to be made against them. Written by Rich. Baxter to prevent the causless dissent and separation of any sincere Christians from our Churches or sincere Ministers from our Associations. Especially for the satisfaction of the inhabitants of Kederminster. London [as before]—Contents on reverse — Treatise pp. 120 — Errata slip pasted on page 120.

*** See 'Reliquiæ' [Lib. I. pp. 112-113] for powerful statement of the occasion of this book.

VI. & VII. The Worcestershire Petition to the Parliament for the Ministry of England Defended, by a Minister of Christ in that Country ; in Answer to XVI. Queries, Printed in a Book, called a Brief Discovery of the three-fold Estate of Anti-Christ : Where unto is added Counter-Queries, and an Humble Monition to Parliament, People, and Ministers.

London, Printed for Tho. Underhill at the Blue Anchor in Paul's Church-yard : and Francis Tyton at the Three Daggers in Fleet Street, 1653, sm. 4°.

Collation: Title-page—the Preface— 4 pp. and pp. 40 [Dated on last page 'March 28, 1653.'] The title-page of the 'Petition' Baxter 'defends' and which he himself drew up, follows :— 'The Humble Petition of many thousands, Gentlemen, Free-holders, and others, of the County of Worcester, To the Parliament of the Common-wealth of England. In behalf of the Able, Faithful, Godly Ministry of this Nation. Delivered by Colonel John Bridges and Mr Thomas Foly, December 22, 1652. With the Parliament's Answer thereunto. London, Printed by Robert White, for Francis Tyton, and Thomas Underhill, and are to be sold at their shops, the three Daggers in Fleet-street, and the Bible and Anchor in Pauls Church-yard, 1652, 4°. Title—and pp. 3–8 [subscribed by above six thousand].

*** In the Williams' Library copy of preceding there is at page 3 in the holograph of Baxter an addition 'omitted in the printing' entitled 'Answer to 2d question'—See 'Reliquiæ' [Lib. I. p. 115] where Baxter avows having drawn up the 'Petition' and notices the want of the addition found in Williams' copy as above: 'by an oversight [it] is maimed by the want of the answer to one of the accuser's queries.' Darling in his 'Cyclopædia Bibliographica' *s.n.* erroneously describes *above* as printed in 'A Brief Discovery of the three-fold state of Anti-Christ" whereas Baxter is defending the 'Petition' from the attack that appeared in this (Quaker?) publication.

VIII. Rich. Baxter's Apology against the modest Exceptions of Mr T. Blake and the Digression of Mr G. Kendall. Whereunto is added Animadversions on a late Dissertation of Ludiomæus Colvinus alias Ludovicus Molinæus M. Dr Oxon. And an Admonition of Mr W. Eyre of Salisbury, with Mr Crandon's Anatomy for satisfaction of Mr Caryl. London, Printed for T. Underhill and F. Tyton, and are to be sold by Is. Nevil at the Plough, and Jos. Barbar at the Lamb in Paul's Church-yard. 1654. [4°]

Collation: Title-page—Epistle Dedicatory to General Edward Whalley pp. 6—A separate title as follows : 'Rich. Baxter's Account given to his reverend brother Mr T. Blake of the Reasons of his Dissent from the Doctrine of his Exceptions in his late Treatise of the Covenants. London, Printed by A. M. for Thomas Underhill at the Anchor and Bible in Paul's Church-yard and Francis Tyton at the three Daggers in Fleet-street 1654'—the Preface Apologetical pp. 14—the Contents pp. 4—Treatise pp. 155—Postscript p. 3. [Often amissing from 'Finis' being on page 155.] A second separate title as follows: 'The Reduction of a Digressor: or Rich. Baxter's Reply to Mr George Kendall's Digression in his Book against Mr Goodwin. London [as before, only added at end after Fleet-street 'near Dunstans Church'] 1654.—Quotations pp. 10—the Contents pp. 8—'Treatise' pp. 144. 'Postscript' pp. 2—Errata and a note 1 page.

Another separate title 'Richard Baxter's Confvtation of a Dissertation for the Justification of Infidels: Written by Ludiomæus Colvinus alias Ludovicus Molinæus, Dr of Physick and History, Professor in Oxford, against his brother Cyrus Molinæus. London, Printed by R. W. Anno Dom. 1654.

'Epistle Dedicatory' to 'my dearly beloved and much honored and valued friend Colonel Sylvanus Taylor,' pp. 7—two short 'notes' 1 page—the Apologetical Preface pp. 6—the Contents pp. 4—the Fragment of an Epistle which was the cause of this Dissertation pp. 6—Treatise 'of the Part of Faith in Justification' pp. 177-326—Another separate title as follows: 'Rich. Baxter's Admonition to Mr William Eyre of Salisbury concerning his Miscarriages in a book lately written for the Justification of Infidels against M. Benj. Woodbridge, M. James Cranford, and the Author. London [as the last]—the Preface pp. 10—the Contents pp. 2—Treatise pp. 40—Note to Reader 1 page—Postcript 1 page —Address to the 'Reader' on 'Mr Crandon's book' — very amusing. Another separate title as follows: — 'An unsavoury Volume of Mr Jo. Crandon's Anatomized, or a Nosegay of the choicest Flowers in that Garden presented to Mr Joseph Caryl by Rich. Baxter. London [as the first separate title-page, *supra*] 1654—To the Reader pp. 3—the Contents pp. 2—To Caryl pp. 3 —Treatise pp. 84.

⁎ My copy bears on the general title-page the autograph of Jonathan Edwardes' Coll. Jesu. Oxon: & Trin. Coll. Dub.'—the famous namesake and precursor of the greater JONATHAN EDWARDS of America. There are singular coincidences of subject in the 'Writings' of the two, and of others of the Edwards' name on this side. See 'Reliquiæ' for BAXTER'S personal notices of his different opponents in this book. [Lib. I. p. 110.] ORME makes five different works out of *above*. Doubtless some of them were issued separately, but the general title-page and continuous pagination, shews BAXTER intended them to form one book.

IX. TRUE CHRISTIANITY or Christ's absolute Dominion and Mans necessary Self-resignation and subjection. In two Assize Sermons preached at Worcester. By Richard Baxter. London, Printed for Nevill Simmons, Booksellar [sic] in Kidderminster, and are to be sold at London by William Roybould at the Unicorne in Pauls Church-yard. 1655. [18°.] There is a separate title-page to each Sermon as follows:

(*a*) A Sermon of the absolute Dominion of God-Redeemer, and the necessity of being devoted and living to him. Preached before the honourable Judge of Assize at Worcester, Aug. 2, 1654. [Rest as in general title.]

(*b*) A Sermon of the absolute Soveraignty of Christ: and the necessity of man's subjection, dependance and chiefest love to him. Preached before the Judges of Assize at Worcester. [Rest as in general title.]

Collation: General title-page — 1st special title-page.—Epistle Dedicatory to 'Serjeant Glyn, now Judge of Assize' pp. 20. Errors 1 page. 1st Sermon from 1 Corinthians vi. 19, 20, pp. 1-116. 2d special title-page. To the Christian reader 2 pp. 2d Sermon from Psalm ii. 10-12, pp 121-216.

⁎ The '*Reliquiæ*' says 'The first was

preached before Judge Atkins, Sir Thomas Rous being high-sheriff: the second before Serjeant Glyn, who desiring me to print it I thought meet to print the former with it.' [As before Pt. I. p. 110.] My copy of this little volume has been successively in the possession of the well-known critics and editors Thomas Park and the Rev. John Mitford. The former's autograph, dated 1815, is on the general title-page: that of the latter on the front fly-leaf, dated Oct. 1840, and he has written 'Two excellent and eloquent sermons.'

X. Rich. Baxter's Confession of his Faith, especially concerning the interest of Repentance and sincere Obedience to Christ in our Justification and Salvation. Written for the satisfaction of the misinformed, the conviction of Calumniators and the Explication and Vindication of some weighty Truths. London, Printed by R. W. for Thos. Underhil and Fra. Tyton, and are to be sold at the Anchor and Bible in Paul's Church-yard, and at the three Daggers in Fleet-street, 1655. [4°.]
Collation: Title-page. 1 page with two quotations. The Preface pp. 47. Contents pp. 3. Errata 1 page. Treatise pp. 462. On page 462 is 'Finis' and here usually copies end: but the complete book has after this 'An Addition to the 11th chapter of the 3d Part of the Saint's Rest' pp. 8 and Letters of the celebrated Gataker pp. 19. Errata 1 page.
*** The last Letter is written by Charles Gataker for his venerable and then dying father. See '*Reliquiæ*' [Lib. I. p. iii] for a very severe and unhappily well-deserved castigation of Dr John Owen, who wrote most unrighteously against both Baxter and John Goodwin. BAXTER in his 'Confession' and in other of his treatises stood side by side with JOHN GOODWIN against the wild Antinomianism of the period.

XI. Humble Advice or the Heads of those things which were offered to many honourable members of Parliament by Mr Richard Baxter at the end of his sermon, December 24 at the Abby in Westminster, with some Additions as they were delivered by him to a friend that desired them, who thought meet to make them publick. London, Printed for Thomas Underhill and Francis Tyton 1655. [4°.]
Collation: Title-page and pp. 11.
*** The British Museum copy has a contemporary date 'Jany 2d.' and the letter 5 in 1655 is marked out and 4 written. Baxter in the 'Reliquiæ' [Lib. I. p. iii] describes this as 'one scrap of a sermon . . . . taken by some one and printed.'

XII. The Vnreasonableness of Infidelity: manifested in Four Discourses, the subject of which is expressed in the next pages. Written for the strengthening of the weak, the establishing of the tempted, the staying of the present Course of Apostasie, and the Recovery of those that have not sinned unto death. By Richard Baxter.
London, Printed by R. W. for Thomas Underhill, at the Bible and Anchor in Paul's Church-yard and for F. Tyton at the 3 daggers in Fleet street. 1655. [12°.]
The following are the 'subjects' referred to in title-page :—

1. The Spirit's extrinsick witness to the Truth of Christianity on Gal. iii. 1-3. With a determination of this Question: Whether the miraculous works of Christ and his Disciples do oblige those to Believe who never saw them? *Aff.*
2. The Spirit's Internal witness to the Truth of Christianity on 1 John v. 10.
3. For Prevention of the unpardonable sin against the Holy Ghost : a Demonstration that the Spirit and works of Christ were the finger of God : or the holy war between Christ and Satan ; on Matt. xii. 22 to 33. A Postscript against Mr Lyford's exceptions.

E

4. The arrogancy of Reason against Divine Revelations repressed: or proud Ignorance the cause of Infidelity and of men's quarrelling with the word of God, on John iii. 9.

Collation: Title-page, Titles as *supra*—a page of passages of Scripture.—Dedication to Lord Broghill pp. 15. An Advertisement pp. 22. The Preface pp. 43. The Contents pp. 10. Errata 1 page. 'The Spirit's Witness' pp. 1-124. Then a separate title-page.

A Determination of this Question, Whether, etc. [as above] London, Printed [as in general title-page] 1655.

To the Reader pp. 2. Treatise pp. 1-195. Another separate title-page:—

For Prevention [as before, down to 'finger of God'] London, Printed Anno Dom. 1655.

Treatise pp. 283. Postscript pp. 284-310. Another separate title-page:—

The Arrogancy [as before] London: Printed by T. N. for Tho. Underhill 1655.

A page of passages of Scripture. Treatise pp. 5-77.

⁎⁎* These several treatises are found separately issued and without Baxter's name on the title-page. In the British Museum Library in the copy of 'The Arrogancy of Reason' there is contemporaneously written on title 'Baxter' and on 'For Prevention, etc., a reference is given to page 82 as determining Baxter to be the author, as follows 'Three or four of these discourses I have spoak of already in my second part of the Saint's Rest.' See 'Reliquiæ' [Lib. I. p. 11] for notice of this very able and acute book. Orme cannot have seen this work or any of the combined treatises.

XIII. *Gildas Salvianus;* the Reformed Pastor. Shewing the nature of the Pastoral work ; especially in private instruction and catechizing. With an open. Confession of our too open sins. Prepared for a day of Humiliation kept at Worcester, December 4 1655 by the ministers of that county who subscribed the agreement for catechizing and personal instruction, at their entrance upon that work. By their unworthy fellow-servant Richard Baxter, Teacher of the Church at Kederminster. London, Printed by Robert White for Nevil Simmons Book-seller at Kederminster, and are to be sold by William Roybould at the Unicorn in Paul's Church-yard. 1656 [12°].

Collation: Title-page—the Preface to 'my reverend and dearly beloved brethren, the faithful ministers of Christ in Brittain and Ireland' pp. 50. To the Lay-Reader pp. 16—quotations from Hammond and Gurnal pp. 4—the Contents pp. 6. Errata 1 page. Treatise [from Acts xx. 28] pp. 480. At end of page 480 is 'Finis. December 25, 1655,' but there follow two Letters (1) 'to the reverend and faithful ministers of Christ in the several counties of this Land, and the gentlemen and other natives of each county now inhabiting the city of London' pp. 7 (2) 'to all the rest of the ministers of the Gospel in this county' pp. 5.

⁎⁎* The second edition, which rapidly followed the first, has an 'Appendix in answer to some Objections which I have heard of, since the .former edition' pp. 60.—[1657]. See 'Reliquiæ' [Lib. I. p. 115] for account of the origin and usefulness of this book.

XIV. The Agreement of divers Ministers of Christ in the County of Worcester and some adjacent parts for Catechizing or personal instructing all in their several Parishes that will consent thereunto. Containing I. The Articles of Agreement. II. An Exhortation to the People to submit to this necessary work. III. The Profession of Faith and Catechism which we desire them first to learn. The second edition. London, Printed by R. W. for Nevil Simmons, Bookseller at Kidderminster and are to be sold there by him and at London by William Raybould at the Unicorn in Paul's church-yard. 1656 [12°].

Collation: This small volume containing Creed, Commandments and a Catechism consists of 42 pages. The former part of 11 pages is subscribed by 58 ministers, of whom Richard Baxter stands first.

*** See 'Reliquiæ' [Lib. I. p. 115]—The Catechism we here learn was an enlargement of a 'Confession' which had been before printed as 'an open sheet' when 'Church-discipline' was 'set up.'

XV. Certain Disputations of Right to Sacraments and the true nature of Visible Christianity: defending them against several sorts of opponents, especially against the second assault of that pious, reverend and dear brother Mr Thomas Blake. By Richard Baxter, Teacher of the Church in Kederminster. London, Printed by William Du-Gard for Thomas Johnson at the Golden Key in St Paul's Church-yard. 1657 [sm. 4°].

Collation: Title-page—On reverse the subjects of the several 'Disputations' —'To the faithfull servants of Christ, the associated ministers of Worcestershire pp. 2—the Preface pp. 32—quotations pp. 3—the Contents pp. 7—Treatise pp. 523—On reverse a quotation from Augustine—Two Postscripts pp. 527-541—Errata pp. 2.

*** Cf. 'Reliquiæ' [Lib. I. pp. 113-114.

XVI. The Quakers Catechism or the Quakers questioned; their Questions answered, and both Published, for the sake of them that have not yet sinned unto death; and of those ungrounded novices that are most in danger of their Seduction. By Richard Baxter.

London, Printed by A. M. for Thomas Underhill at the Anchor and Bible in Paul's Church-yard and Francis Tyton at the Three Daggers in Fleetstreet. 1657. [4°].

Collation: Title-page, and texts on reverse—To the Reader pp. 3—To the Separatists and Anabaptists in England pp. 6—'An Answer to a young unsettled Friend' pp. 11—The Information of George Coolishey, etc. pp. 4 [all unpaged]—Answer pp. 32.

*** See 'Reliquiæ' [Lib. I. p. 116] for an incisive 'rebuke' of the Quakers in connection with this 'Catechism.'

XVII. The Safe Religion or Three Disputations for the Reformed Catholike Religion against Popery. Proving that Popery is against the Holy Scriptures, the Unity of the Catholike Church, the consent of the Antient Doctors, the plainest Reason and common judgement of sense itself. By Richard Baxter.

London, Printed by Abraham Miller, for Thomas Underhill at the Anchor and Bible in Paul's Church-yard and Francis Tyton at the three Daggers in Fleet-street. 1657 [thick 12°.]

Collation: Title-page—To the Protestant Reader pp. 10—To the Literate Romanists that will read this Book pp. 37—the Contents pp. 4—Errata 1 page—Treatise pp. 455—Table pp. 13 [the last often awanting].

*** See 'Reliquiæ.' [Lib. I. pp. 116].

XVIII. A Treatise of Conversion. Preached and now published for the use of those that are strangers to a true Conversion, especially the grossly ignorant and ungodly. By Richard Baxter, Teacher of the Church of Christ at Kederminster. London, Printed by R. W. for Nevil Simmons, Bookseller in Kiderminster, and are to be sold by Joseph Nevil at the Plough in Paul's Church-yard. 1657 [sm. 4°].

Collation: Title-page—Epistle Dedicatory to the inhabitants of Kiderminster pp. 10—To the Reader pp. 6—the Contents, pp. 6—Errata 1 page—Treatise [on Matthew xviii. 3?] pp. 307.

*** See 'Reliquiæ.' [Lib. I. pp. 114]. 'I published a treatise of Conversion, being some plain Sermons on that subject, which Mr Baldwin—an honest young minister that had lived in my house and learned my proper characters or short-hand in which I wrote my sermon-notes—had transcribed out of my notes,' etc. etc.

XIX. A Winding-sheet for Popery. By Richard Baxter, CATHOLICK.
London, Printed by Robert White, for Nevil Simmons, Bookseller in Kederminster, Anno Dom. 1657. [12°].

Collation: Title-page—and pp. 13.
⁎ See 'Reliquiæ' [Lib. I. p. 116].

XX. One Sheet for the Ministry against the Malignants of all sorts. By Richard Baxter.
London, Printed by Robert White, for Nevil Simmons, Bookseller in Kederminster, Anno Dom. 1657. [12°].

Collation: Title-page—and pp. 14.
⁎ See 'Reliquiæ' [Lib. I. p. 117].

XXI. One Sheet against the Quakers. By Richard Baxter.
London, Printed by Robert White for Nevil Simmons, Bookseller in Kederminster, Anno Dom. 1657. [12°].

Collation: Title-page—Treatise pp. 13.
⁎ See 'Reliquiæ' [Lib. I. p. 116].

XXII. A Second Sheet for the Ministry justifying our Calling against Quakers, Seekers and Papists, and all that deny us to be the Ministers of Christ. By Richard Baxter. London, Printed by R. White for Nevil Simmons, Bookseller in Kidderminster. 1657. [sm. 4°].

Collation: Title-page—and pp. 16.
⁎ See 'Reliquiæ' [Lib. I. p. 117].

XXIII. Directions to Justices of Peace, especially in Corporations, for the discharge of their duty to God: written at the request of a Magistrate, and published for the use of others yt need it. By *Richard Baxter*, impelled by the love of God and men to become their submissive Monitor. London, Printed by Robert White for Nevil Simmons. 1657. [12°].

⁎ *Collation:* Half-title—and pp. 7. My copy is a contemporary MS. dated 'Octob. 20. 1657'—and looks like the *holograph* of Baxter. I purchased it in Worcester along with a number of Baxter's rarest tractates. In the 'Reliquiæ' [Lib. I. p. 117] he says 'I printed it in an open sheet to stick upon a wall.'

XXIV. A Call to the Unconverted to Turn and Live and Accept of Mercy while Mercy may be had, as ever they would find mercy in the day of their extremity: From the Living God. By his unworthy servant Richard Baxter, to be read in families where any are unconverted. The eleventh edition. London, Printed by R. W. for N. Simmons, Bookseller at Kederminster and are to be sold by Henry Mortlock at the sign of the Phœnix in St Paul's Church-yard, 1665. At 1s. bound [18°].

Collation: Title-page. The Reason of this work pp. 4. The Preface pp. 32. Contents pp. 4. Books by Baxter pp. 4 [all unpaged]. Treatise pp. 239. [Text Ezekiel xxxiii. 11].

⁎ Among many editions I have selected that of the year of the plague '1665.' We can well understand the wistfulness with which *then* he would re-issue it. The 13th edition '1669' has the 'addition of some passages.' The first edition was published in 1657. It at once seized the popular heart and has never lost its hold. It is perhaps the most vital of all Baxter's books. See his 'Reliquiæ' [Lib. I. pp. 114-115], for his own wondering and grateful account of its 'unexpected success.' 'I had rather,' said Dr Isaac Watts, 'be the author of Mr Baxter's "Call to the Unconverted" than the author of Milton's Paradise Lost.' In common with other of Baxter's writings it imparts its own unearthly fervour—as Henry Rogers has noted—to the many great minds who have written of it. Cf. Rogers' splendid 'Essay' prefixed to the modern reprint of Baxter's 'Practical Works' [4 vols. impl. 8vo. 1838], and Dr Chalmers' 'Introduction to the 'Call' and 'Now or Never' in Collins' series. It was soon translated into nearly every language of Europe. I was shewn at Harvard University Library, Cambridge U. S. a copy of a version by holy John Eliot the Apostle of the Indians into their strange tongue; which with the Bible is the one pathetic monument of a nation and language long since extinct.

COTTON MATHER in his Life of Eliot tells very tenderly of one of the Indian chiefs dying with the 'Call' as his one light as he travelled towards the setting Sun.

XXV. RICHARD BAXTER'S Account of his present Thoughts concerning the Controversies about the Perseverance of the Saints. Occasioned by the gross misreports of some passages in his book, called The Right Method for Peace of Conscience, etc.; which are left out in the last impression to avoid offence, and this here substituted, for the fuller explication of the same points. London, Printed for Tho. Underhill at the Anchor and Bible in Paul's Church-yard and F. Tyton at the Three Daggers in Fleet-street. 1657 [4°].

Collation: Title - page.—Treatise pp. 42.

*** On the title-page of my copy is the autograph of the good 'John Billingsley' 1687. See 'Reliquiæ' [Lib. I. p. 110] for autobiographic references in connection with this tractate.

XXVI. Making Light of Christ and Salvation too oft the issue of Gospel - Invitations. Manifested in a sermon preached at Laurence Iury in London. By Rich. Baxter, Teacher of the Church of Christ at Kederminster, in Worcestershire. London, Printed by R. White for Nevil Simmons Bookseller in Kederminster, 1658 12° [Text Matthew xxii. 5]. Title-page. To the Reader pp. 4. Treatise pp. 181-243.

*** In the 'Reliquiæ' there is a singularly interesting account of the original 'preaching' of this Sermon : and as it evidences his popularity and power it follows 'This Sermon was preached at Laurence Iury, where Mr Vines was pastor: where though I sent the day before to secure room for the Lord Broghill and the Earl of Suffolk, with whom I was to go in the coach : yet when I came the crowd had so little respect of persons that they were fain to go home again because they could not come within hearing : and the old-Earl of Warwick who stood in the abbey) brought me home again. And Mr Vines himself was fain to get up into the pulpit and sit behind me and I to stand between his legs: which I mention that the reader may understand that verse in my poem concerning him which is printed, where I say

'At once the pulpit held us both' [Lib. I. s. 112.]

XXVII. A Sermon of Judgement, Preached at Pauls before the Honourable Lord Maior and Aldermen of the City of London, Decemb. 17, 1654. And now enlarged. By Rich. Baxter. London, Printed by R. W. for Nevil Simmons, Bookseller in Kederminster, 1658. 12°.

Collation: Title-page—Dedication 'To the Right Honourable Christopher Pack, Lord Maior of London, with the right worshipful Aldermen' pp. 11—To the ignorant or careless reader pp. 3—Treatise pp. 174 [Text 2 Corinthians v. 10, 11].

*** My copy has on the front fly-leaf the autograph of the excellent 'John Rawlet'—[Nos. xxvi. and xxvii. make one volume, with continuous pagination]. I have another edition of this little book by itself '1672.' 'Another of these Sermons [as preached in London] which I published was 'a Sermon of Judgment, which I enlarged into a small treatise. This was preached at Paul's [St Paul's] at the desire of Sir Christopher Pack, then Lord Mayor, *to the greatest auditory that I ever saw.*' 'Reliquiæ' [Lib. I. p. 112].

XXVIII. The Crucifying of the World by the Cross of Christ. With a Preface to the Nobles, gentlemen and all the rich, directing them how they may be richer. By Richard Baxter. London, Printed by R. W. for Nevill Simmons, Bookseller in Kederminster, and are to be sold by him there ; and by Nathaniel Ekins at the Gun in Paul's Church-yard. Anno Dom. 1658 [4°].

Collation: Title-page—Epistle Dedicatory 'to my worthy friend, Thomas Foley, Esq.' pp. 6—the Preface pp. 50 —quotations from Baronius, etc., pp. 6—

the Contents pp. 6—books of same author pp. 2 — Treatise pp. 254 —[The 'Text' on which it is based is Galatians vi. 14.]

⁎ See 'Reliquiæ' [Lib. I. p. 116.] It has been recently admirably re-printed under the careful editorship of Mr Baillie the biographer of Hewitson.

XXIX. Of Saving Faith: that it is not only gradually but specifically distinct from all common faith. The Agreement of Richard Baxter with that very learned consenting adversary that hath maintained my assertion by a pretended confutation in the end of Sergeant Shephard's book of Sincerity and Hypocrisie. With ten Reasons of my Dissent in some passages that came in on the by. London, Printed by R. W. for Nevill Simmons Bookseller in Kederminster, and are to be sold by him there; and by Nathaniel Ekins at the Gun in Paul's Churchyard. Anno Dom. 1658 [4°].

Collation: Title-page—Epistle to Sergeant S. pp. 2—Contents pp. 3—errata on reverse of p. 3—Treatise pp. 96.

⁎ 'Finis' is placed on page 89 and on page 90 this Note: 'Reader, Because many that have bought the former editions of my book called the *Saint's Rest*, do grudge that I have annexed a sheet to the 7th impression on this subject which was not in the former, that they may have it here without buying that book again, I shall here also annex it.' It fills pp. 90–96.—In the 'Reliquiæ' [Lib. I. p. 117] Baxter refers to Bishop Barlow's part in Sergeant Shephard's book: and complains bitterly of the Printer for having done his work so 'shamefully that it is scarcely to be understood.'

XXX. Confirmation and Restauration, the necessary means of Reformation and Reconciliation: for the Healing of the Corruptions and Divisions of the Churches: Submissively, but earnestly tendered to the consideration of the Soveraigne Powers, Magistrates, Ministers and People, that they may awake and be up and doing in the execution of so much as appeareth to be necessary, as they are true to Christ, His Church and Gospel, and to their own and other souls, and to the peace and wellfare of the Nations; and as they will answer the neglect to Christ at their peril.

By Richard Baxter, an unworthy Minister of Christ, that longeth to see the healing of the Churches. London, Printed by A. M. for Nevill Simmons, Bookseller in Kederminster, and are to be sold by Joseph Cranford, at the Kings-Head in Pauls Church-yard. 1658. [12°.]

Collation: Title-page—To the Reader pp. 9—The Contents pp. 18—Treatise 316—Postscript [unpaged] p. 64—Errata 1 page.

⁎ This book was highly commended by Dr Patrick, late Bishop of Ely, in his *Aqua Genitalis* p. 471. Calamy Account Vol. I. p. 413. All Patrick's references to Baxter are respectful and kindly. See the recent collective edition of his Works by Taylor, *sub nomine*. Cf. also 'Reliquiæ' [Lib. I. p. 117].

XXXI. The Judgment and Advice of the Assembly of the Associated Ministers of Worcester-shire, held at Worcester Aug. 6th 1658. Concerning the endeavours of Ecclesiastical Peace and the waies and means of Christian unity, which Mr John Durey doth present; sent unto him in the name, and by the appointment of the aforesaid Assembly. By Richard Baxter Pastor of the Church at Kederminster. London, Printed for T. Underhill at the three Daggers in Fleet-street, 1658 [4°].

Collation: Title-page—and pp. 2–8. Inscription 'To my reverend and much honoured brother Mr John Durey'... See 'Reliquiæ' [Lib. I. pp. 117] where Baxter states that besides *above*, he 'drew up in Latin more largely' a 'judgment' how best to expedite 'Pacification.'

XXXII. Of Justification: Four Disputations clearing and amicably defending the Truth against the unnecessary oppositions of divers learned and reverend brethren. By Richard Baxter, a servant of Christ for Truth and Peace. London, Printed by R. W. for Nevil Simmons, Bookseller in Kederminster and are to be sold by him there; and by Nathanal Ekins at the Gun in Pauls Churchyard, 1658 [4°]

Collation: Title-page — the Preface pp. 12 — the Contents pp. 6 — Errata 1 page — Treatise pp. 423.
*** See 'Reliquiæ' [Lib. I. p. 14] for account of this — He there says 'If the Reader would have the sum of my judgment about justification in brief, he may find it very plainly in a sermon on that subject among the 'Morning Exercises at St Giles in the Fields, preached by my worthy friend Mr Gibbons of Black-Fryers — in whose church I ended my public ministry,' etc. etc.

XXXIII. Directions and Perswasions to a Sound Conversion: For Prevention of that Deceit and Damnation of Souls, and of those Scandals, Heresies and desperate Apostasies, that are the consequents of a Counterfeit or Superficial Change. By Richard Baxter. London, Printed by A. M. for Nevil Simmons, Bookseller in Kederminster, and are to be sold by him there, and by N. Ekins, at the Gun in Paul's Church-yard, 1658 [12°].

Collation: Title-page — The Preface pp. 8 — The Contents pp. 4 — Errata — Treatise pp. 534 — 'Which book hath been marvellously useful to many, and, by preventing those mistakes in practical religion which are often fatal,' Calamy: Account, Vol. I. p. 413. See also 'Reliquiæ' [Lib. I. p. 115].

XXXIV. The Grotian Religion Discovered, at the Invitation of Mr Thomas Pierce in his Vindication. With a Preface, vindicating the Synod of Dort from the calumnies of the New Tilenus; and David, Peter, etc. And the Puritanes and Sequestrations, etc., from the censures of Mr Pierce. By Richard Baxter, Catholick. London, Printed by R. W. for Nevill Simmons, Bookseller in Kederminster, and are to be sold by him there, and by Tho. Brewster, at the three Bibles, and by John Starkey at the Miter at the West end of Paul's, 1658 [18°].

Collation: Title-page — Errata — The Preface pp. 51 — Books by Baxter pp. 2 — Treatise pp. 119.
*** At commencement of this Treatise Baxter has printed 'April 9, 1658, *Incept*,' and at close 'Finitur, April 14, 1658,' an example of his extraordinary rapidity of composition. 'Written against Dr Pierce containing a vindication of the doctrine of the Synod of Dort and the old Puritans,' Calamy, 'Account,' Vol. I. p. 413. Cf. Baxter's own full and passionate account: Reliquiæ, Baxt. [Lib. I. p. 113.] He says 'It was only the matter of fact which I undertook, viz., to prove that Grotius profest himself a moderate Papist: but for his fault in so doing I little meddled with it.'

XXXV. Five Disputations of Church-Government and Worship. I. Whether it be necessary or profitable to the right order or peace of the Churches of England, that we restore the extruded Episcopacy? Neg. II. Assert. Those who nullifie our present ministry and Churches which have not the prelatical ordination, and teach the people to do the like, do incur the guilt of grievous sin. III. An Episcopacy desirable for the Reformation, Preservation and Peace of the Churches. IV. Whether a stinted Liturgie or Form of Worship be a desirable means for the peace of these Churches? V. Whether human ceremonies be necessary or profitable to the Church? By Richard Baxter. London, Printed by R. W. for Nevil Simmons, Bookseller in Kederminster, and are to be sold by him there and by Thomas Johnson at the Golden Key in St

Paul's Church-yard, 1659. At 4s. 6d. bound [sm. 4°].

Collation: Title-page—Epistle Dedicatory 'To his Highness Richard, Lord Protector' pp. 8—a Preface pp. 38—the Contents pp. 8—Errata 1 page—an Advertisement to prevent misunderstanding pp. 24—Treatise pp. 492—On page 491 is added 'Finitur. July 9, 1658,' and then 'Satisfaction to certain Calumniators'—This refers to a charge that he was making 'three or four hundred a-year' by his books—with curious details as to the prices of books and publishing arrangements. Baxter with great vigour rebukes his 'slanderers' pp. 491-492.

The following are the separate title-pages of each part :—

I. Only a heading as follows, 'Whether it be necessary or profitable to the right order or the peace of the Churches of England that we restore the extruded Episcopacy?'

II. The Second Disputation vindicating the Protestant Churches and ministers that have not prelatical ordination, from the reproaches of those dividers that would nullify them. Written upon the sad complaints of many godly ministers in several parts of the nation, whose hearers are turning Separatists. By Richard Baxter. London, Printed by Robert White for Nevil Simmons, Bookseller in Kederminster. 1658.

III. The Third Disputation for such sorts of Episcopacy or Disparity in exercise of the ministry, as is desirable or conducible to the peace and reformation of the Churches. [As before].

IV. The Fourth Disputation of a Form of Liturgy : how far it is necessary, desirable or warrantable : in order to a Peace between the Parties that differ herein, and too uncharitably prosecute their difference. [As before].

V. The Fifth Disputation of humane ceremonies whether they are necessary or profitable to the Church, and how far they may be imposed or observed ? By Richard Baxter. London [as before].

⁎ 'A book pleading for moderation at the time when bishops, liturgy and ceremonies were most decried and opposed.' Calamy 'Account' Vol. I. p. 413. See Baxter's own fuller statement in 'Reliquiæ' [Lib. I. pp. 117, 118].

XXXVI. A Key for Catholicks to open the Jugling of the Jesuits and satisfie all that are but truly willing to understand, whether the cause of the Roman or Reformed Churches be of God ; and to leave the reader utterly unexcusable that after this will be a Papist. The first Part, containing some Arguments by which the meanest may see the vanity of Popery ; and 40 Detections of their Fraud ; with Directions and Materials sufficient for the Confutation of their voluminous deceits: particularly repelling Boverius, Richlieu, H. T.'s Manual, some Manuscripts, etc. With some Proposals for a (hopeless) Peace. The second Part sheweth (especially against the French and Grotians) that the Catholick Church is not united in any meerly humane head, either Pope or Council. By Richard Baxter, a Catholick Christian and Pastor of a Church of such at Kederminster. London, Printed by R. W. for Nevil Simmons, Bookseller in Kederminster, and are to be sold by him there, and by Thomas Johnson at the Golden Key in St Paul's Church-yard. 1659. At 4s. bound [sm. 4°].

Collation: Title-page — the Preface pp. 18—the Contents pp. 19-26—Errata 1 page—Treatise pp. 459—On pp. 459-60 the 'Satisfaction to certain Calumniators' referred to under No. XXXV.

⁎ At the close of 'the Preface' he thanks, of all men, the 'Earl of Lauderdale' for having 'translated' his French 'quotations' for him ! In 1674 Baxter published a 2d edition of the 'Key' which is described as 'much corrected and augmented.' See 'Reliquiæ' [Lib. I. p. 118] for a powerful statement of the circumstances under which the 'Key'

Writings of Richard Baxter.

was written, even 'at the hazard of his life.'—Cf. also 'Reliquiæ' p. 180. It has been well edited and republished by Allport.

XXXVII. A Holy Commonwealth or Political Aphorisms opening the true Principles of Government: for the healing of the mistakes and resolving the doubts that most endanger and trouble England at this time (if yet there may be hope). And directing the Desires of sober Christians that long to see the Kingdoms of this world become the Kingdoms of the Lord and of his Christ. Written by Richard Baxter at the invitation of James Harrington, Esquire. With a Preface to them that have caused our eclipses since 1646, and a sounder Answer to the Healing Question, and the Jesuits Method for restoring Popery. London, Printed for Thomas Underhill and Francis Tyton, and are to be sold at the sign of the Anchor and Bible in Paul's Church-yard and at the Three Daggers in Fleet-street. 1659. [Cr. 8vo.]

Collation: Title-page — the Preface pp. 28—an addition pp. 44—Adam Coutzen the Jesuites Directions for preserving and restoring Popery, and changing Religion in a Nation before the people are awake pp. 13—the Contents pp. 6—Treatise pp. 517—catalogue of the Publishers' books pp. 9—On reverse of last page, 'To the Binder' and this note, 'The price of this book is 3s. bound.'
⁎⁎ See the 'Reliquiæ' [Lib. I. pp. 118, 119] for a full account of this very remarkable book — also onward [Part III. pp. 71, 72] where he assigns his reasons for recalling it and asking it to be regarded as *non scriptum*.

XXXVIII. A Treatise of Self-Denial. By Richard Baxter, Pastor of the Church at Kederminster. London, Printed by Robert White, for Nevil Simmons at the Princes Arms in Saint Pauls Church-yard. 1675 [cr. 8°].

Collation: Title-page. A Premonition concerning this Second Edition, pp. 4. Epistle Dedicatory to Colonel James Berry, etc. pp. 38 [entitled 'The Epistle Monitory']. The Preface, pp. 39. The Contents, pp. 11 [all unpaged]. Treatise pp. 417. A Dialogue of Self-Denial (in verse) pp. 13 [unpaged]. Text [Luke ix. 23, 24.]
⁎⁎ The Dialogue is often awanting. The following is the title, etc. of the original edition :—

A Treatise of Self-Denyall. By Richard Baxter, Pastor of the Church at Kederminster. London, Printed by Robert White, for Nevil Simmons, Bookseller in Kederminster, and are to be sold by him there, and by William Gilbertson at the Bible in Gilt Spur-street without Newgate, and by Joseph Nevil at the Plow in Pauls Church-yard, 1660. At 3s. 3d. bound. [sm. 4°.]

Collation: Title-page. Epistle Dedicatory to Berry [as above] pp. 30. The Preface, pp. 30. The Contents, pp. 5 and on reverse of page 5 'Errata.' Treatise [from Luke ix. 23, 24] pp. 329. A 'Dialogue' pp. 8. As noted above from 'Finis' being placed on page 329 this 'Dialogue' which is added, unpaged, is often amissing.
⁎⁎ See 'Reliquiæ' [Lib. I. p. 117].

XXXIX. Catholick Unity: or the only way to bring us all to be of one Religion. By Rich. Baxter. To be read by such as are offended at the differences in Religion and are willing to do their part to heal them.

London, Printed by R. W. for Thomas Underhill and Francis Tyton, and are to be sold at the sign of the Anchor and Bible in Paul's Church-yard, and at the three Daggers in Fleet Street. 1660. [18°].

Collation: Title-page. Dedication 'To all those in the severall Parishes of these Nations that complain of the disagreements in matters of Religion' pp. 29. The Contents, pp. 4. Treatise, pp. 379. On last page this note 'Preached Dec. 24th 1657.
⁎⁎ 'Another Sermon which I preached at Martin's Church, I printed with enlargement called Catholick Unity.' 'Reliquiæ' [Lib. I. p. 112]. Text, Ephesians iv. 3.

XL Universal Concord. The first Part. The sufficient Terms proposed for the use of those who have the liberty to use them : and as the Author's Profession of his own Religion in a contentious, dividing age. By Richard Baxter. The First and General Part is preparatory to the Second Part, containing the Particular Terms of Reconciling the severall differing Parties that are Reconcileable. London, Printed by R. W. for Nevil Simmons, Bookseller in Kederminster. 1660. [12°].

Collation: Title-page—to the Reader pp. 10. Treatise, pp. 80.

⁎⁎* The only copy of this that I have anywhere traced is in the Bodleian, acquired since the printed Catalogue was prepared. From the 'Reliquiæ' [Lib. I. pp. 119, 120], we learn that above was all that was published. 'When I wrote I thought to have published a second part . . . . . but the change of the times hath necessarily changed that purpose.' Calamy assigns it to 1658: so that he can't have seen it; nor ORME who copies 1658. It is difficult to account for its extreme scarcity. Others preceding the Fire of London are frequently to be found.

XLI. The True Catholick and Catholick Church described and the vanity of the Papists and all other Schismaticks that confine the Catholick Church to their sect discovered and shamed. By Richard Baxter, a member of that one Universal Church which containeth all the true Christians in the world. With an apologetical Postscript against the factions principles and writings of Mr T. Malpas, Mr T. Pierce, Philo-Tilenus and such others.—London, Printed by A. M. for T. Underhill at the Anchor and Bible in Pauls Church yard, and F. Tyton at the three Daggers in Fleetstreet. 1660 [18°].

Collation: Title-page — the Preface pp. 6—Contents pp. 4—Treatise [from 1 Corinthians xii. 12] pp. 275—Postscript pp. 277–331—Errata on reverse of page 331.

⁎⁎* See 'Reliquiæ' [Lib. I. p. 112] for a stirring account of the design of this book and a pungent notice of 'Malpas'—ORME misdates this 1659.

XLII. A Sermon of Repentance, preached before the Honourable House of Commons assembled in Parliament at Westminster at their late solemn Fast for the settling of these Nations, April 30, 1660. By Richard Baxter. London, Printed by R. W. and A. M. for Francis Tyton and Jane Underhill, and are to be sold at the sign of the three Daggers in Fleetstreet and at the Bible and Anchor in Pauls Church-yard. 1660 [4°].

Collation: Title-page—To House of Commons pp. 4—Sermon [Text xxxvi. 31] pp. 47.

⁎⁎* 'Reliquiæ' [Lib. I. p. 120].

XLIII. Right Rejoycing : or the Nature and Order of rational and warrantable joy. Discovered in a Sermon preached at St Pauls before the Lord Maior [sic] and aldermen, and the several companies of the city of London on May 10, 1660, appointed by both Houses of Parliament to be a day of solemn Thanksgiving for God's raising up and succeeding his Excellency and other instruments, in order to his Majestie's restoration and the settlement of these Nations. By Richard Baxter. London, Printed by R. W. and A. M. for Francis Tyton and Jane Underhill, and are to be sold at the sign of the three Daggers in Fleetstreet and at the Bible and Anchor in Paul's Church-yard. 1660 [4°.]

Collation: Fly-leaf 'request of the court for the sermon'—Title-page—Epistle Dedicatory to Lord Mayor,' etc. pp. 4—Sermon [Luke x. 20] pp. 51.

⁎⁎* 'Reliquiæ' [Lib. I. p. 120].

XLIV. The Life of Faith, as it is the Evidence of things unseen. A Sermon preached [contractedly] before the King at White-Hall upon July the 22th [sic] 1660. By Richard Baxter, one of his Majesties Chaplains in Ordinary. Published by his Majestie's special Command. With enlargement, and relaxation of the style for common use. London, Printed by R. W. and A. M. for Francis Tyton and Jane Underhill, and are to be sold at the three Daggers in Fleet-street and at the Bible and Anchor in Pauls Church-yard; and by Nevil Simmons at Kederminster. 1660. [4°].

Collation: Title-page — Address to 'Readers' 1 page—Sermon pp. 68 [Text, Hebrews xi. 1.]

*** This was subsequently very much enlarged and re-published as virtually a new book—See No. LIX.: 'Reliquiæ' [Lib. I. p. 120].

XLV. The Successive Visibility of the Church of Which the Protestants are the soundest Members. I. Defended against the Opposition of Mr William Johnson. II. Proved by many Arguments. By Richard Baxter. Whereto is added 1. An Account of my judgement to Mr J. how far Hereticks are or are not in the Church. 2. Mr J.'s Explication of the most used terms; with my Queries thereupon and his Answers, and my Reply. 3. An Appendix about successive Ordination. 4. Letters between me and T. S. a Papist, with a Narrative of the Success. London, Printed by R. W. for Nevil Simmons, Bookseller in Kederminster, and are to be sold by Francis Tyton at the three Daggers in Fleet-street. 1660 [12°].

Collation: Title-page—The Preface and Postscript pp. 1–28—The Contents pp. 6—Errata—Treatise pp. 392.

*** This Treatise has the following separate title-pages :—

At page 194 'The Second Part: Wherein the successive Visibility of the Church, of which the Protestants are chief Members, is clearly proved: And the Papists exception against it confuted. London, Printed in the year 1660.

At page 308 'Mr Johnson's Explication of Some of the most used Terms, with Queries thereupon: and his Answer and my Reply. London, Printed 1660.

At page 362 'A Letter Written to Thomas Smith a Papist, concerning the Church of Rome. London, Printed 1660.

See 'Reliquiæ' [Lib. I. p. 119] for account of this book.

XLVI. The Vain Religion of the Formal Hypocrite and the mischief of an unbridled tongue (as against religion, rulers or dissenters) described in several sermons, preached at the Abby [sic] in Westminster before many members of the Honourable House of Commons. 1660. And the Fool's Prosperity, the occasion of his destruction : a Sermon preached at Coven-Garden [sic]. Both published to heal the effects of some hearers' misunderstandings and mis-reports. By Richard Baxter. London, Printed by R. W. for F. Tyton at the three daggers in Fleet-street, and Nevel Simmons Bookseller at Kederminster. 1660. At 1s. bound. [18°.]

Collation: Title-page—To the Reader pp. 7]—Postscript pp. 3—Contents pp. 5 —Treatise pp. 271 ['Text' James i. 26] —A separate title as follows: 'The Fool's Prosperity.' A Sermon preached at Coven-Garden: published upon occasion of some offence and mis-reports By R. B. Printed in the year 1660— [Text Proverbs i. 32, 33]—Treatise pp. 275–340.

*** 'Reliquiæ' [Lib. I. p. 120].

XLVII. A Petition for Peace : with the Reformation of the Li-

turgy. As it was Presented to the Right Reverend Bishops by the Divines appointed by His Majesties Commission to treat with them about the alteration of it. London, Printed Anno Dom., 1661 [4°].
Title-page—Petition pp. 1-21—'The Reformation,' pp. 22-102.
₊ On this in the 'Reliquiæ,' Baxter says 'After our Dispute at the Savoy somebody printed our Papers (most of them) given in to them in that Treaty: of which the Petition for Peace, the Reformed Liturgy (except the Prayer for the King which Dr W. wrote) the large reply to their Answer of our Exceptions, and the last two Addresses, were my writing. But in the first Proposals and the Exceptions against the Liturgy I had less to do than others' [Lib. I. p. 121]. ORME again over-extends his List by making two distinct books of this tractate. The following relates to the same:—

An Accompt of all the Proceedings of the Commissioners of both Perswasions appointed by His sacred Majesty, according to Letters Patents, for the Review of the Book of Common Prayer.
⁕London, Printed for R. H., 1661 [4°].
Collation: Title-page—A copy of his Majesty's commission 6 pp. [unpaged] and pp. 35—Documents, 2 pp. [unpaged] and pp. 128.

XLVIII. The Mischiefs of Self-Ignorance and the Benefits of Self-Acquaintance: Opened in divers Sermons at Dunstan's-West. And Published in answer to the Accusations of some and the Desires of others. By Richard Baxter.
London, Printed by R. White for F. Tyton, at the three daggers in Fleet-street, 1662, at 2s. 6d. bound [12°].
Collation: Title-page—Epistle Dedicatory to Anne Countess of Balcarres [sic] with a Postscript pp. 46—Another to 'my dearly beloved the inhabitants of the Burrough and Parish of Kederminster in Worcestershire,' pp. 12—Contents pp. 10—Errata 1 page—Treatise pp. 504—(Text 2 Cor. xiii. 5) 'Catalogue of Books written and published by the same Author,' pp. 4.
₊ 'Reliquiæ' [Lib. I. p. 120.]

XLIX. RICHARD BAXTER, his Account to his dearly beloved the inhabitants of Kidderminster of the causes of his being forbidden by the Bishop of Worcester to preach within his Diocess. With the Bishop of Worcester's Letter in Answer thereunto. And some short Animadversions upon the said Bishop's Letter. London, Printed Anno Dom. 1662 [4°].
Collation: Title-page—'To my dearly beloved the inhabitants of the Burrough and Parish of Kederminster in Worcester-shire' pp. 6 [unpaged] in the Bishop of Worcester's Letter pp. 118—the Attestation of Dr Gunning and Dr Pearson concerning a command of lawful superiors, what was sufficient to its being a lawful command, page 19—the Postscript pp. 20-26 [but pages 25 and 26 mispaged 31 and 32 — a letter unto a person of honour and quality containing Animadversions upon the Bishop of Worcester's Letter pp. 33—41 signed D. E. [continued mis-printing of the pages on from page 25] a 'Second Letter' pp. 42-45 also signed D. E. and a curious little 'postscript' on J. C. m. d. page 45.
₊ Never was a 'Dignitary' of any Church so mercilessly handled. Baxter is here specially terse and pungent in his style, and has occasional gleams of admirable humour.—The Address to his Kidderminster 'friends' is very pathetic and intensely earnest.

L. A Saint or a Brute. The certain Necessity and Excellency of Holiness, etc. So plainly proved and urgently applied, as by the blessing of God may convince and save the miserable, impenitent, ungodly sensualists, if they will not let the Devil hinder them from a sober and serious reading and considering. To be communicated by the charitable, that desire the conversion and salvation of souls, while the patience of God and the day of grace and hope continue. By Richard Baxter. The First Part: shewing the necessity of Holiness. London, Printed by R. W. for

Francis Tyton, at the three daggers in Fleet-street, and Nevil Simmons, Bookseller at Kederminster, Anno Dom. 1662 [4°].

Collation: Title-page—Dedication 'to my dearly beloved Friends, the inhabitants of Kederminster,' etc. pp. 9—The Contents [of both Parts] pp. 5—The Introduction pp. 23 [separate pagination] Treatise [from Luke x. 41, 42] pp. 98—A second title as follows:—'A Saint or a Brute. The Second Part. Clearly proving by Reason as well as Scripture, 1. In general that Holiness is best and necessary to our felicity : 2. Particularly that it is best, 1. For Societies, 2. For individual persons. And more distinctly, 1. That it is the only way of safety : 2. Of honesty : 3. The most graceful way : 4. The most honourable : 5. The most pleasant. And therefore to be chosen by all that will obey true reason and be happy. London, Printed Anno Dom. 1662.' Treatise [same text] pp. 101-384.

LI. Besides the 'Farewell Sermon' [No. CXXVI.] there is another in all the Collections of the 'Ejected's' Farewell Sermons. In my copy of the famous quarto of 1663, it follows Jenkyn's, and fills 24 pages—' Preached August 17, 1662.' The text is Colossians ii. 6, 7.

LII. Fair Warning : or XXV. Reasons against Toleration and Indulgence of Popery ; with the Arch-Bishop of Canterbury's Letter to the King and all the Bishops of Ireland's Protestation to the Parliament to the same purpose. With an Answer to the Roman Catholicks reasons for Indulgence. Also the Excellent Reasons of the Honourable House of Commons against Indulgence ; with Historical Observations thereupon. London, Printed for S. U. N. T. F. S. 1663 [4°].

Collation: Title-page — Letter [as above] pp. 2—Protestation [as above] pp. 2—Appeal [signed John Wigorn] pp. 2—Twenty-five Reasons pp. 1-23 [signed Richard Baxter, Catholique]—Answer [as above] pp. 23-32—The excellent Reasons [as above] pp. 33-39.

⁎⁎ This is also found as follows :—

A Word in Season. Or, The Great Plot for Restoring Popery by Opposing all Settlement and Uniformity, Foreseen by the Orthodox, Confessed by the Nonconformists ; and managed by the Jesuits, as evidently appears by their own several following words :
1. To Remove all Jealousies of the present Government and Religion.
2. To justifie to all sober and honest Catholicks who are not herein concerned, the present great care and laws against Popery.
3. And to reclaime all godly Men from those courses against Government that they know and confesse have given, and do give the greatest advantage to Popery. With Serious Considerations to those multitudes of late inclined to Popery : and XL. Godly Remedies against it.
London, Printed for William Squire, 1663. [4°]

Title-page—and pp. 55 'Finis' being placed on pp. 55 : but thereafter is an 'Appendix' mis-paged 49–60, then 73–76, 'Finis' being again placed on p. 76 and 'Richard Baxter, Catholique' immediately beside. To this impression there is this general title-page—

Fair Warning. First and Second Part. To which is added a Third. By the Direction of the same Person.
London, Printed for S. T. V. T. 1663 [4°].

ORME makes two distinct works of *above,* drawing his description from Hallam's Constitutional History,' *s. n.*

LIII. The Divine Life : in three Treatises : the first, Of the Knowledge of God ; the second, Of Walking with God ; the third, Of Conversing with God in Solitude. By Richard Baxter. London, Printed for Francis Tyton at the three Daggers in Fleet-street, and Nevil Simmons Bookseller in Kederminster. 1664 [sm. 4°].

Collation: Title-page — Special title for first part as follows:—'A Treatise of the Knowledge of God and the impression which it must make upon the heart; and its necessary effects upon our lives. Upon John xvii. 3.' By Richard Baxter. London [as before]—Epistle Dedicatory 'to the right honourable and exemplary lady Ann, countess of Balcarres' pp. 9—to the Reader pp. 2—the Contents pp. 4—Errata at bottom of fourth page—Treatise pp. 151. A special title for second part as follows:—'The Description, Reasons and Reward of the Believers Walking with God. On Gen. v. 24.' By Richard Baxter. London [as before] —the Contents pp. 3—Treatise pp. 159-291. A special title for third part as follows:—'The Christians converse with God: or the Insufficiency and Uncertainty of Humane Friendship and the Improvement of Solitude in Converse with God. With some of the author's breathings after him. By Richard Baxter. London [as before]—the Contents pp. 2—Treatise [on John xvi. 32] pp. 297—[misprinted 379]—379. My copy has the autograph of Romaine on the front flyleaf.

⁎ The general title-page is often awanting. See 'Reliquiæ' [Lib. I. pp. 120-121] for very interesting autobiographic account of this book: and of the portion which 'the Bishop's chaplain' caused to be expunged.'

LIV. Below [No. LV.] is a 'Second Sheet.' I have not been able to find a copy of the 'First Sheet.' It is thus described in the 'Reliquiæ' [Lib. I. p. 122.] 'I wrote two sheets for poor Families: the first containing the method and motives for the conversion of the ungodly.' ORME makes the 'Two Sheets' one publication. The 'Reliquiæ' *supra* shews this to be incorrect.

LV. The Second Sheet for Poor Families. Instructions for a Holy Life. By Richard Baxter. London, Printed by Robert White, for Francis Tyton at the three Dragons in Fleet-street: and for Nevil Simmons Bookseller in Kederminster. 1665. [12°].

Collation: Title—and 14 pp.: dated 'May 10, 1665.'

⁎ On my copy there is written on the title-page 'By Subscription at the London Coffee-house' undated. See 'Reliquiæ' [Lib. I. p. 122].

LVI. The Reasons of the Christian Religion. The first Part of Godliness: proving by natural evidence the Being of God, the necessity of Holiness and a future life of Retribution; the sinfulness of the world; the desert of hell; and what hope of recovery mercies intimate. The second Part of Christianity: Proving by Evidence super-natural and natural, the certain truth of the Christian Belief; and answering the Objections of Unbelievers. First meditated for the well-setting of his own belief, and now published for the benefit of others, by Richard Baxter. It openeth also the true Resolution of the Christian Faith. Also an Appendix defending the soul's immortality against the Somatists and Epicureans and other Pseudo-philosophers. London, Printed by R. White for Fran. Titon at the three Daggers in Fleet-street. 1667. [4°].

Collation: Title-page—To the Christian Reader pp. 8—To the doubting and the unbelieving readers pp. 7—To the hypocrite readers pp. 7—the Contents pp. 7—Errata 1 page—Treatise pp. 604.

⁎ The 'Reliquiæ' [Part III. p. 61] gives the occasion of this lucid and unanswerable book, which anticipates nearly all vaunted modern objections — and refutes them.

LVII. Directions for Weak distempered Christians to Grow up to a confirmed State of Grace. With Motives opening the lamentable Effects of their Weaknesses and Distempers. The First Part. Published also to further that Repentance which Wars, and

Plagues and Flames and Church-Convulsions, have so long and loudly Preached to England. By Richard Baxter. London, Printed for Nevil Simmons at the Three Crowns over against Holborn Conduit. 1669 [12°].

Collation: Title-page—Epistle Dedicatory to Church at Kederminster pp. 3—The Preface pp. 13—The Contents pp. 2—Treatise pp. 158.

⁂ 'Reliquiæ' [Part III. p. 61]. 'This book came forth when I was in prison, being long before refused by Mr Grigg.'

LVIII. The Character of a Sound Confirmed Christian, as also 2. Of a Weak Christian; and 3. Of a Seeming Christian. Written to imprint upon men's minds the true Idea or (conception) of Godliness and Christianity. By Richard Baxter. The Second Part of the Directions for Weak Christians.

London, Printed by R. White for Nevil Simmons at the Three Crowns near Holborn Conduit. 1669. [12°].

Collation: Title-page—To the Reader pp. 7—Contents pp. 7—Treatise pp. 183.

⁂ 'Reliquiæ' as in LV.

LIX. THE LIFE OF FAITH. In three parts. The first is a sermon on Hebrews xi. 1, formerly preached before his Majesty, and published by his command; with another added for the fuller application. The second is Instructions for confirming believers in the Christian Faith. The third is Directions how to live by faith or how to exercise it upon all occasions. By Richard Baxter. London, Printed by R. W. for Nevil Simmons at the three crowns over against Holborn Conduit. 1670. [4°].

Collation: Portrait of Baxter 'Ætat 55, 1670' with long love-locks, moustache and imperial—curious engraved title-page (a reduction of that prefixed to the 'Saint's Everlasting Rest'). [See No.

II. (7).]—Title-page as *supra* — Epistle Dedicatory 'to the worshipfull, my much honoured friend, Richard Hampden of Hampden Esquire and the Lady Lætitia, his wife' pp. 6—the Preface pp. 4—the Contents pp. 5—Errata 1 page, wherein 'the first and great errour of the printer is that he hath not distinguished the three distinct parts'—another Epistle or Address to the Reader asking his 'Holy Commonwealth' for reasons assigned, to be regarded as *non-scriptum* [See No. XLIV.] pp. 2—Treatise pp. 607—a catalogue of books written and published by the same author and other books published by Simmons pp. 4.

⁂ See 'Reliquiæ' [Part III. p. 61].

LX. The Cure of Church-divisions: or Directions for weak Christians to keep them from being Dividers or Troublers of the Church. With some Directions to the Pastors how to deal with such Christians. By Richard Baxter. London, Printed by Nevil Simmons at the three crowns over against Holborn-Conduit. 1670 [thick 12°].

Collation: Title-page—The Author's purpose, reasons and prognostics pp. 34—Abstract of the directions pp. 12—Treatise pp. 430—Violence, Love and Separation contrasted in three columns pp. 5—Errata 1 page—books by Baxter, etc. p. 6.

⁂ In 'Reliquiæ' [Part III. pp. 70, 71] will be found account of a lamentable dispute between the booksellers [or Publishers]: wherein BAXTER shews that when he elected to use it he had rare sarcastic power and even humour — See also p. 72.

LXI. A Defence of the Princiciples of Love which are necessary to the unity and concord of Christians; and are delivered in a book called the Cure of Church-Divisions. I. Inviting all sound and sober Christians (by what name soever called) to receive each other to communion in the same Churches. II. And when that (which is first desirable) cannot be obtained, to bear with each other in their distinct Assemblies and to manage them all in Christian love. Written to detect and eradicate all love-killing, dividing and Church-destroying principles, passions and practices, and to preserve the weak in this hour of manifold temptations. By Richard Baxter, one of the Mourners for a self-dividing and self-afflicting Land. London, Printed for Nevill Simmons at the sign of the three Crowns near Holborn Conduit. 1671 [cr. 8°].

Collation: Title-page — quotations from Calvin pp. 4—Contents pp. 8—the Preface 'to those Readers who are of the Exceptor's mind and are offended at my book called the Cure of Church-Divisions, pp. 22—Then a separate title as follows: 'The General Part or Introduction to the Defence of my Cure of Church-Divisions, being a Narrative of those late actions which have occasioned the offence of men in both extremes; with the true reasons of them, and of those writings which some account unreasonable: with the true stating of the Case of that Separation which my opposed treatise meddleth with: and an answer to several great objections. Printed in the year 1671—pp. 25-104—Part II. pp. 1-150—Postscript pp. 151-183.

⁂ See 'Reliquiæ' [Part III. p. 73] for account of the reception of No. LXI.: and of the occasion of this 'Defence.' Again Dr Owen acted most disingenuously—Darling misunderstanding CALAMY gives two 'Defences' for this one.

LXII. Now or Never. The Holy, Serious, Diligent Believer justified, encouraged, excited and directed. And the Opposers and Neglecters convinced by the light of Scripture and Reason. By Richard Baxter. To be communicated by such as want ability or opportunity themselves to plead the cause of Serious Holiness, for men's conviction.
London, Printed by R. W. for F. Tyton, at the three Daggers in Fleet-street, and Nevil Simmons at the three Crowns near Holborn Conduit. 1671 [18°].

Collation: Title-page—The Preface pp. 37—The Contents pp. 6—Treatise pp. 240.

⁂ A quaint little edition was published at Edinburgh immediately. 'Printed by Andrew Anderson, and are to be sold at his house on the north side of the street fore-gainst the Cross. Anno Dom. 1672 [18°].

LXII. The Divine Appointment of the Lord's Day proved: as a separated day for holy Worship; especially in the Church Assemblies. And consequently the cessation of the seventh day Sabbath. Written for the satisfaction of some religious persons who were lately drawn into error or doubting in both these points. By Richard Baxter. London, Printed for Nevil Simmons at the three Crowns near Holborn Conduit. 1671 [cr. 8°].

Collation: Title-page—the Contents pp. 6—Treatise pp. 153. There follows: 'An Appendix for further Confirmation of God's own Separation of the Lord's Day, and disproving of the Jewish seventh day Sabbath. Written since the Treatise went to the Press, upon the invitations of some latter objections. London [as before]—pp. 157-227—Postscript pp. 229-237.

⁂ 'Reliquiæ' [Part III. p. 74.]

LXIV. The Duty of Heavenly Meditation reviewed by Richard Baxter at the invitation of Mr Giles Firmin's Exceptions, in his book entitled The Real Christian. London, Printed for Nevil Simmons at the sign of the three crowns near Holborn-conduit. 1671 [4°].

Collation: Title-page—Treatise pp. 33.

⁂ 'Reliquiæ' [Part III. p. 74.]

LXV. How far Holinesse is the Design of Christianity. Where the Nature of Holiness and Morality is opened and the Doctrine of Justification, Imputation of Sin and Righteousness, etc., partly cleared and vindicated from abuse. In certain Propositions returned to an unknown Person, referring to Mr Fowler's Treatise on this subject. London, Printed for Nevil Simmons at the Three Crowns at Holborn Conduit. 1671 [4°].

Collation: Title-page and pp. 24—At bottom of p. 22 date 'Aug. 24 (the fatal day) 1671.' On p. 23 'What Happiness is.' 'What Holiness or virtue is.' On p. 24 'Holiness not fanatically proud or aspiring.'

⁂ See 'Reliquiæ' [Part III. p. 85] for notice of Fowler—BAXTER excels in these etchings or sketches of character.

LXVI. The Difference between the Power of Magistrates and Church-Pastors and the Roman Kingdom and Magistracy under the name of a Church and Church-Government usurped by the Pope or liberally given him by Popish Princes: Opened by Richard Baxter. To the Learned and sincere Ludovicus Molinœus Dr of Physick and Author of Jugulum Causæ, Papa Ultrajectinus, and other books on this subject. For the Vindication of the true Pastoral Discipline exercised by the ancient Churches and claimed but alas! too little exercised, by the Churches Protestant and Reformed. And to acquaint Posterity what we hold in this, that false accusations misinform them not. London, Printed for Nevil Simmons at the sign of the three Crowns near Holborn Conduit. 1671. [4°].

Collation: Title-page—To the Reader pp. 2. Treatise pp. 59.

⁂ See 'Reliquiæ' [Part III. p. 85] for a characteristic notice of the occasion of this treatise.

LXVII. God's Goodness Vindicated. For the help of such (especially in Melancholy) as are Tempted to deny it and think him Cruel because of the Present and Future Misery of Mankind: With respect to the Doctrine of Reprobation and Damnation. By Richard Baxter. Published and Prefaced by a Friend at whose desire it was Written and to whom it was Committed.

London, Printed for N. Simmons at the three Crowns near Holborn Conduit. 1671. [sm. 18°].

Collation: Title-page. The Publisher to the Reader pp. 4. Treatise pp. 99.

⁂ There is no text: but on the title-page 1 John iv. 16. This is extremely rare. The 'friend' was the famous John Corbet. See 'Reliquiæ' [Part III. p. 85].

LXVIII. A Second Admonition to Mr Edward Bagshaw: Written to call him to Repentance for many false doctrines, crimes, and specially fourscore palpable untruths in matter of fact, deliberately published by him in two small libels; in which he exemplifieth the love-killing and depraving principles of Church-dividers: and telleth the world to what men are hasting, when they sinfully avoid Communion with true Churches and Christians for tolerable faults. With a Confutation of his Reasons for Separation: Written to preserve the weak, to resist the dividing temptations of the imperious, unskilful clergy, to revive our dying hopes of Concord and to vindicate the Nonconformable ministers from the unjust imputation of schismatical principles. By Richard Baxter, a long maligned and resisted endeavourer of the Churches unity and peace. London, Printed for Nevill Simmons at the Three Crowns near Holborn Conduit. 1671. [8°].

Collation: Title-page. Contents pp. 7. Treatise pp. 188. Postscript pp. 188–190. fly-leaf 1 page about misquotation on Cromwell.

⁂ See 'Reliquiæ' [Part III. p. 85 on Bagshaw.

LXIX. More Reasons for the Christian Religion and No Reason against it. Or a Second Appendix to the Reasons of the Christian Religion, Being

 I. An Answer to a Letter from an unknown Person, charging the Holy Scriptures with Contradictions.
 II. Some Animadversions on a Tractate *De Veritate*,

F

written by the noble and learned Lord Edward Herbert, Baron of Chizbury [sic] etc. and printed at Paris 1624 and at London 1633. Resolving Twelve Questions about Christianity. By Richard Baxter. London, Printed for Nevil Simmons at the Princes Arms in St Pauls Churchyard, 1672. [18°].

Collation: Title-page. Epistle Dedicatory 'To the Right Worshipful Sir Henry Herbert, Kt. etc.' 4 pp.—and pp. 172. 'Errata' on fly-leaf.

⁎ The 'Epistle Dedicatory' being addressed to the brother of Lord Herbert Baxter writes very lovingly of the family, especially of the 'excellently holy as well as learned and ingenious a person Mr George Herbert orator to the University of Cambridge and a faithful Pastor in the English Church.' He praises much in the *De Veritate:* and he thus closes 'I may well suppose that your approbation of the cause I plead for will make it needless to me to apologize for my boldness in meddling much with such an Author, while I do it with all tenderness of his deserved honour.' The 'Letter' from the 'unknown person' is given pp. 1–7. It is signed 'Your loving Friend in the Bond of Peace.' The alleged difficulties adduced relate to the apparently discrepant accounts of the Resurrection of our Lord. Baxter replies with much sagacity and insight and more terseness than was common with him—adducing Hammond and other authorities with fine catholicity of appreciation. See 'Reliquiæ' [Part III. p. 90].

LXX. A Treatise of Death the Last Enemy to be destroyed. Shewing wherein its enmity consisteth and how it is destroyed. Part of it was preached at the Funeral of Elizabeth the late wife of Mr Joseph Baker, Pastor of the Church at Saint Andrews in Worcester. By Rich. Baxter. With some few passages of the life of the said Mrs Baker observed. London, Printed for Nevil Simmons at the Princes Arms in St Pauls Churchyard 1672. [12°].

Collation: Title-page. Epistle Dedicatory to Mayor etc. of Worcester, pp. 32. Contents pp. 3. Treatise [on 1 Corinthians xv. 26] pp. 143. 'Some suitable passages of the life of Mrs Baker' pp. 144–159.

⁎ See 'Reliquiæ' [Lib. I. p. 120].

LXXI. Sacrilegious Desertion of the holy ministery rebuked and tolerated preaching of the Gospel vindicated, against the reasonings of a confident Questionest in a book called [Toleration not to be abused] with Counsel to the Nonconformists and Petition to the Pious Conformists. By one that is consecrated to the Sacred Ministery and is resolved not to be a wilful deserter of it, in trust that any undertakers can justifie him for such desertion at the judgment of God ; till he knew better how those can come off themselves who are unfaithful Pastors or unjust Silencers of others. Printed in the year, 1672 [12°].

Collation: Title-page — Treatise pp. 139—On the reverse of page 139 a few errata.

⁎ See 'Reliquiæ [Part III. p. 102]— Extremely rare : and historically important as shewing the ground-principle whereon the 'Ejected' rested in refusing to cease the exercise of their function as 'Preachers.'

LXXII. The Certainty of Christianity without Popery : or whether the Catholick Protestant or the Papist have the surer faith. Being an Answer to one of the oft canted questions and challenges of the Papists, sent to one who desired this. Published to direct the unskilful how to defend their faith againt Papists and Infidels, but especially against the Temptations of the Devil, that by saving their Faith they may save their Holiness, their Comfort and their souls. By Richard Baxter. London, Printed by Nevil Simons at the Sign of the Prince's Arms in St Paul's Church-yard, 1672 [12°].

Collation: Title-page—Address to the Protestant Reader pp. 3—Paper 'from an unknown person in a letter,' pp. 6—Contents pp. 3—Treatise pp. 112.
*** See 'Reliquiæ' [Part III. pp. 99].

LXXIII. The Church Told of Mr Ed. Bagshaw's Scandals and Warned of the dangerous snares of Satan now laid for them in his Love-Killing Principles: With a farther proof that it is our common duty to keep up the interest of the Christian Religion, and Protestant Cause in the Parish Churches, and not to imprison them by a confinement to tolerated meetings alone. By Richard Baxter, a Militant Servant of Christ for Faith, Hope, and Love, Unity, Concord, and Peace, against their contraries on both extremes.

London, Printed in the year 1672 [4°].

Collation: Title-page and Errata on reverse—pp 32.
*** The following from the 'Reliquiæ' [Part III, p. 89] is interesting—'Mr Bagshaw—in his rash and ignorant zeal, thinking it a sin to hear a Conformist, and that the way to deal with the persecutors was to draw all the people as far away from them as we could, and not to hold any communion with any that did conform—having printed his third reviling libel against me, called for my third Reply which I entitled "The Church Told," etc. But being printed without licence, L'Estrange the Searcher, suppressed part of it in the press—there being lately greater penalties laid on them that print without a licence than ever before —And about the day that it came out Mr Bagshaw died—a prisoner though not in prison: which made it grievous to me to think that I would seem to write against the dead. *While we wrangle here in the dark, we are dying and passing to the world that will decide all our controversies:* and the safest passage thither is by peaceable holiness.'

LXXIV. A Christian Directory: or a Summ of Practical Theologie and Cases of Conscience. Directing Christians how to use their Knowledge and Faith; how to improve all Helps and Means and to perform all Duties; how to overcome Temptations and to escape or mortifie every Sin. In Four Parts, I. Christian Ethicks (or private Duties) II. Christian Oeconomicks (or Family Duties) III. Christian Ecclesiesticks (or Church Duties) IV. Christian Politicks (or Duties to our Rulers and Neighbours). By Richard Baxter. London, Printed by Robert White for Nevill Simmons at the sign of the Princes Arms in St Paul's Church-yard, 1673, [folio].

Collation: Prefixed is the curious emblematical title-page as *ante*.—Title-page — Advertisements [*i.e.* Preface] pp. 7—Contents pp. 21—an alphabetical Table and and Errata pp. 15—There are separate titles as follows:—

1. A Christian Directory. The First Part: Christian Ethicks or Directions for the ordering of the private actions of our hearts and lives in the work of holy self-government unto and under God. By Richard Baxter. London, Printed by Robert White for Nevill Simmons at the Three Crowns near Holborn Conduit 1672 — Title and pp. 469.

2. A Christian Directory or a Sum of Practical Divinity. The Second Part: viz. Christian Oeconomicks; or the Family Directory, containing Directions for the true practice of all duties belonging to Family relations, with the Appurtenances. By Richard Baxter. London [as in the general title-page]—Title and pp. 475-667.

3. A Christian Directory. The Third Part. Christian Ecclesiasticks: or Directions to Pastors and People about sacred doctrine, worship and discipline and their mutual duties. With the solution of a multitude of Church-controversies and cases of conscience. By Richard Baxter. London [as the last] Title—Note 1 page and pp. 673-929.

4. A Christian Directory or a Summ of Practical Divinity by way of Direction. The Fourth Part. Christian Politicks: containing all the duties of the six last commandments in our political relations and towards our neighbours. With the principal Cases of Conscience about them. By Richard Baxter. London [as the last] Title—Epistle pp. 2 and pp. 214 — Advertisements [to Readers] pp. 8, giving account of the Books, signed 'a most unworthy servant of so good a Master'— Contents of all pp. 19— Errata 1 page.

⁎ Joseph Thompson Esq. Ardwick, Manchester has in his fine Collection a copy of above work which from the crowns (in gold) and initials appears to have been in the possession of Charles II. It is a fine copy in full red morocco and has White's portrait from the 'Reliquiæ,' prefixed. A 'second' edition was published in 1678.—A comparison of the pagination, etc. shews it to have been a re-print and not a mere re-issue.—'The most complete ['Directory'] that is extant in the English language or perhaps in any other.' Calamy, 'Account,' Vol. I. p. 416. See 'Reliquiæ,' [Part III. p. 61].

LXXV. Short Instructions for the Sick, Especially for the [who by] Contagion or otherwise are deprived of the Presence of a faithful Pastor. By Richard Baxter. 1673. A folio broad-sheet. At the bottom 'This was written in the time of the great plague 1665 for the sick in the city of London: but because it is the work of all our lives to prepare for a safe and comfortable death it is reprinted for the use of all. 1673.'

⁎ British Museum copy has by a contemporary 'for the' erazed and 'who by' inserted, as *supra*. Query 'those?' See 'Reliquiæ' [Lib. I. p. 121].

LXXVI. Full and Easy Satisfaction which is the True and Safe Religion. In a Conference between D. a Doubter, P. a Papist and R. a Reformed Catholick Christian. In Four Parts.
i. The true stating of our Difference and opening what each Religion is:
ii. The true, easie and full Justification of the Reformed or Protestant Religion.
iii. The Protestant's Reasons and Charges against Popery enumerated.
iv. The first Charge, viz., Against Transubstantiation made good: In which Popery is proved to be the Shame of Humane Nature, notoriously contrary to Sense, Reason, Scripture and Tradition, or the Judgment of the Antient and the Present Church; devised by Satan to expose Christianity to the Scorn of Infidels. By Richard Baxter.
London, Printed for Nev. Simmons at the Princes Arms in St. Pauls Church-yard. 1674. [cr. 8°].

Collation: Title-page. Epistle Dedicatory to the Duke of Lauderdail [*sic*] pp. 13. To the Reader pp. 3. The Contents and Errata pp. 4. pp. 189.

⁎ On back of p. 189 is a notice that 'the First Part of the Key for Catholicks being re-printed' is intended 'to be bound' with the above, as 'the chief part of the book.' See 'Reliquiæ' [Part III. p. 107] for a fuller account.

LXXVII. The Poor Man's Family Book.
i. Teaching him how to become a true Christian.
ii. How to live as a Christian, towards God, himself and others, in all his relations; especially in his Family.
iii. How to die as a Christian in Hope and Comfort, and so to be Glorified with Christ for ever. In plain, familiar Conferences between a Teacher and a Learner. Written by Rich. Baxter. With a request to Landlords and Rich men to give to their Tenants and poor Neighbours, either this or some fitter Book.

London, Printed by R. W. for Nevill Simmons at the Sign of the Prince's Arms in St Paul's Churchyard. 1674. [12°].
Collation: Title-page. A Request to the Rich pp. 2. To the Reader pp. 3. The Contents pp 6. Treatise pp. 423. Forms of Prayer etc. pp. 117 [but a mispagination after page 100, 97 being repeated thereafter and the further pagination reckoned therefrom.]
⁎⁎* I have the '5th edn.' which bears to be 'corrected by the Author, with the additions of some hymns,' 1684. 'Reliquiæ' [Part III. p. 147].

LXXVIII. AN APPEAL to the Light or Richard Baxter's Account of four accused passages of a Sermon on Eph. i. 3 published in hope either to procure the convincing instructions of the wise or to humble and stop the erroneous resisters of the truth. Read Joh. 3. 20, 21 and Jam. 3. London, Printed for Nevil Simmons at the Princes-Arms in St Paul's Churchyard, 1674 [sm. 4°).
Collation: Title - page — 'Appeal' pp. 6.
⁎⁎* On page 6 is this 'Postscript' which reminds us of Bunyan's like complaints, 'I must here tell the world that there are divers sheets published and cryed about as mine: with my name prefixed: as *one* called Mr Baxter's Directions for Family Duties; another of Sentences about Conversion, and more such, which are none of mine, but are falsely so pretended, to my wrong: some said to be printed by John Coniers in Southwark, and some by others.' See 'Reliquiæ' [Part III. p. 154].

LXXIX. RICHARD BAXTER'S Catholick Theologie: plain, pure, peaceable: for Pacification of the dogmatical Word-Warriours who 1. By contending about things unrevealed or not understood 2. and by taking verbal differences for real, and their arbitrary notions for necessary sacred truths, deceived and deceiving by ambiguous unexplained WORDS, have long been the shame of the Christian Religion, a scandal and hardning to unbelievers, the incendiaries, dividers and distracters of the Church, the occasion of State discords and wars, the corrupters of the Christian Faith and the subverters of their own souls and their followers, calling them to a blind zeal and wrathful warfare against true piety, love and peace, and teaching them to censure, backbite, slander, and prate against each other, for things which they never understood. In three books. I. Pacifying principles about God's decrees, foreknowledge, Providence, operations, redemption, grace, man's power, free-will, justification, merits, certainty of salvation, perseverance, etc. II. A pacifying praxis or dialogue about the five articles, justification, etc. proving that men here contend almost only about ambiguous words and unrevealed things. III. Pacifying disputations against some real errors which hinder reconciliation viz. about physical predetermination, original sin, the extent of redemption, sufficient grace, imputation of righteousness, etc. Written chiefly for Posterity, when sad experience hath taught men to hate theological logical wars, and to love, and sue, and call for peace. (Ex Bello Pax). London, Printed by Robert White for Nevill Simmons at the Princes Arms in St Pauls Churchyard. 1675 [folio].
Collation: Title-page — Quotations pp. 5—the Preface pp. 26—'Table' of 'Divisions and Contentions of Christians 1 page. Then a separate title-page as follows: — 'Catholick Theologie: The first Book. Pacifying Principles collected from the common notices of Nature, the certain Oracles of God in the Holy Scriptures and the common consent of Christians. For the reconciling of the Church-dividing and destroying Controversies, especially about Predestination, Providence, Grace and Freewill, Redemption, Justification, Faith, Merit, Works, Certainty of Salvation, Perseverance, and many others. In three Parts. I. Of God's nature, know-

ledge, decrees (and Providence about sin, with man's free-will as the objects of the former). II. Of God's government and moral works. III. Of God's operations on man's soul. By Richard Baxter, an earnest desirer of the unity, love and peace, of Christians: for endeavouring of which he expecteth with resolved patience, still to undergo the censures, slanders and cruelties of ignorance, pride and malice, from all that are possessed by the 'wisdom and zeal which are from beneath, earthly, sensual and devilish, the causes of confusion and every evil work. James iii. 14, 15, 16. London [as in *general* title-page]. Then a third title-page—

(*a*) The First Part: Of the Nature, Relations, Knowledge and Decrees of God and of Free-Will and Providence as the Objects thereof. Such selected Verities as are needful to reconcile the common Differences about Predestination, Providence, Grace and Free Will; between the Synodists and Arminians, Calvinists and Lutherans, Dominicans and Jesuits, etc. By Richard Baxter. London [as before].

General title-page to 1st Book *supra* (1)—Separate title-page to 1st Part—The Contents pp. 2—Errata 1 page—pp. 136. Then—

(*b*) The Second Part: Of God's Government and Moral Works. Wherein of his laws or Covenants, of Redemption, of sufficient and effectual Grace, of Faith, Justification, Works, Merits, Perseverance, certainty of Salvation, etc. so far as the Church-troubling-Controversies do require. London [as before].

Separate title—The Contents pp. 2—A Premonition pp. 26—Appendix to this Premonition pp. 4 [unpaged]—pp. 27–124. Then—

(*c*) The Third Part: Of God's Gracious Operations on Man's Soul; their Difference and the Operations of Man's Will. For the fuller Decision of the Controversies about Effectual and Dif- ferencing Grace. By Richard Baxter.

London [as before].

Separate title—The Contents pp. 2—pp. 118. Then—

Catholick Theology: The Second Book. The Synodists and Arminians, Calvinists and Lutherans, Dominicans and Jesuits Reconciled. Or An End of the Controversies about God's Decrees and Grace and Man's Free Will, Merit, &c. if men are willing. A Retreat to the Militant Divines who have too long warred about words and unrevealed things; and kept the Church of God in Flames and drawn Christ's Members to hate, reproach and persecute each other for they knew not what. In a Dialogue between C. (a Calvinist) A. (an Arminian) and B. (the Reconciler): and others. By Richard Baxter.

London [as before].

Separate title—The Contents 5 —pp. 299.

*** See 'Reliquiæ' [Part III. p. 181] for notice of this 'matter-full' book.

LXXX. More Proofs of Infants Church-Membership and consequently their right to Baptism: or a Second Defence of our infant rights and mercies. In three parts. The first is, The plain proof of God's statute or covenant for infants Church-membership from the Creation, and the continuance of it till the institution of Baptism; with the Defence of that proof against the frivolous exceptions of Mr Tombes. And a Confutation of Mr Tombes, his arguments against Infants Church-membership. The second is, A Confutation of the strange forgeries of Mr H. Danvers against the antiquity of infant baptism and of his many calumnies against myself and writings. With a catalogue of fifty-six new commandments and doctrines which he and the sectaries who joyn with him in those calumnies seem to own. The third part is Animadversions on Mr Danver's Reply to Mr Wilks. Extorted by their urgent importunity from an earnest desirer of the love and peace of all true Christians. By Richard Baxter. London, Printed for N. Simmons at the Princes Arms and J. Robinson at the Golden Lyon in St Pauls Church-yard. 1675. [8°].

Collation: Title-page — the Preface pp. 4—Contents pp. 8—Treatise pp. 414. At close of page 414 is a curious notice of the 'hawkers' crying B.'s books 'under his window' as *ante*—book advt.
*** See 'Reliquiæ' [Part III. p. 187] where Baxter describes above as consisting of a 'few sheets' whereas it is a considerable volume.

LXXXI. In the different editions of the 'Morning Exercise against Popery' [1675] the 5th Sermon is by Baxter 'Against any meer Humane Head of the Church of Christ, either Personal or Collective.'

LXXXII. Two Disputations of Original Sin. I. Of original sin. II. Of original sin, as from our neerer parents. Written long ago for a more private use; and now published—with a Preface—upon the invitation of Dr T. Tullie. By Richard Baxter. London, Printed for Robert Gibbs at the Golden Ball in Chancery-Lane, 1675 [12°].

Collation: Title-page — 'To the impartial friends of sacred truth pp. 64—Treatise pp. 65-245.

LXXXIII. Select Arguments and Reasons against Popery. By R. Baxter. London, Printed in the year 1675. [4°].

Collation: Title-page—pp. 6.
*** The only copy of this tract that I have found is in 'Sion College' Library.

LXXXIV. A Treatise of Justifying Righteousness. In Two Books: I. A Treatise of Imputed Righteousness, opening and defending the True Sense, and confuting the False, with many of Dr Tullie's Reasonings against Truth, Peace and Me: With an Answer to Dr Tullie's Letter adjoyned. II. A Friendly Debate with the Learned and Worthy Mr Christopher Cartwright, containing 1. His Animadversions on my Aphorisms with my Answer. 2. His Exceptions against that Answer. 3. My Reply to the Summe of the Controversies agitated in those Exceptions. All Published instead of a fuller Answer to the Assaults in Dr Tullie's *Justificatio Paulina*, for the quieting of Censorious and Dividing Contenders, who raise odious Reports of their Brethren as Popish etc. who do but attempt Reconcilingly to open this Doctrine more clearly than themselves. By Richard Baxter. London, Printed for Nevil Simons and Jonath. Robinson at the Prince's-Arms and Golden-Lion in St Paul's Church-yard. 1676. [cr. 8°].

Collation: Title-page—To the Readers pp. 14.

There are separate titles as follows:—

(1.) Of the Imputation of Christ's Righteousness to Believers: in what sence sound Protestants hold it; and of the false devised sence by which Libertines subvert the Gospel. With an Answer to some common Objections, especially of Dr Thomas Tully whose Justif. Paulina occasioneth the publication of this. By Richard Baxter a compassionate Lamenter of the Churches wounds caused by hasty judging and undigested conceptions and by the theological wars which are hereby raised and managed; by perswading the world that meer verbal or notional differences are material and such as our faith, love, concord and communion must be measured by, for want of an exact discussion of the ambiguity of words. London [as before]—the Preface pp. 15. Contents pp. 2. Treatise pp. 198.

(2.) An Answer to Dr Tullies angry Letter. By Richard Baxter. London [as before] pp. 94—errata pp. 2. Without a separate title but headed.

(3.) 'May 26, 1652.' 'An account of my Consideration of the friendly, modest, learned Animadversions of Mr Chr. Cartwright of York, on my Aphorisms' pp. 294. Postscript pp. 8.

(4.) The Substance of Mr Cartwright's Exceptions considered. By Rich. Baxter. London [as before]—pp. 3–69. Postscript on Mr Danvers pp. 70–79.

LXXXV. Rich. Baxter's Review of the State of Christians Infants. Whether they should be entered in the Covenant with God by Baptism and be visible members of His Church and have any Covenant-right to pardon and salvation? or Whether Christ, the Saviour of the World, hath shut all mankind out of His visible Kingdom and covenant-rights and hopes till they come to age? And whether he did so from the beginning of the world or after his incarnation? Occasioned by the importunity of Mr E. Hutchinson (and of Mr Danvers and Mr Tombes) who called him to this Review in order to his Retractation. An unpartial reading is humbly requested of those dissenters who would not be found despisers of holy truth nor such as judge before they hear. London, Printed for Nevil Simons at the Princes Arms in Pauls Churchyard. 1676. [cr. 8°.]

Collation: Title-page—To the Reader pp. 6. Treatise pp. 64.
⁎ See 'Reliquiæ' [Part III. p. 187.]

LXXXVI. The Judgment of Nonconformists of the Interest of Reason in matters of Religion, in which it is proved against Makebates that both Conformists and Nonconformists and all parties if true Protestants are herein really agreed though unskilful speakers differ in words. London, Printed in the year 1676. [4°.]

Collation: Title-page and pp. 21.
⁎¹ On page 21 is the following 'We whose names are subscribed, not undertaking for any individual person who is otherminded, do ourselves believe the real concord of Protestants as it is here expressed. Thomas Manton, William Bates, Rich. Baxter, Thos. Case, Mat. Sylvester, Edward Lawrence, etc., etc.' In the Williams Library copy there are added in MS. 'Gabriel Sangor, Heny. Hurst, Roger Morice.'

LXXXVII. The Judgment of Nonconformists of Things Indifferent commanded by Authority, as far as the Subscribers are acquainted with it. Written to save the ignorant from the temptations of Diabolism (described 2 Tim. 3. 3 and 1 John 3. 10, 12, 15. John 8. 44). Printed in the year 1676. [4°.]

Collation: Title-page—Treatise pp. 21–41. (continued pagination from No. LXXXV).

LXXXVIII. The Judgment of Nonconformists of Things sinful by Accident and of Scandal, published to save Men's Souls from the Guilt of believing those Men who tell them that the Nonconformists asserted that Whatever may be the occasion of sin to any must be taken away or that Nothing may be imposed which Men may take Scandal at or by Accident turn to sin. And to help those to Repentance who have polluted their Souls with Falshood and Uncharitableness by relieving them and seconding their Reports. Printed in the Year 1676. [4°.]

Collation: Title-page—Treatise pp. 43–79 (continued pagination from No. LXXXVII.)

LXXXIX. What Meer Nonconformity is not: the Profession of Several whom these Times have made and called Nonconformists. Printed in the Year 1676. [4°.]

Collation: Title-page—Treatise pp. 81-123. (continued pagination from LXXXVIII).

XC. Roman Tradition Examined as it is urged as Infallible against all men's senses, reason, the Holy Scripture, the tradition and present judgment of the far greatest part of the Universal Church in the point of Transubstantiation, in answer to a book called a Rational Discourse of Transubstantiation. Printed in the year 1676 [4°].

Collation: Title-page—Treatise pp. 73—a 'Postcript' being on pp. 72, 73.

XCI. A Supplement to the Morning-Exercise at Cripplegate: or several more Cases of Conscience practically resolved by sundry ministers. London, Printed for Thomas Cockerill at the sign of the Atlas in Cornhil near the Royal Exchange. 1676 [4°].

Sermon XXII. 'What light must shine in our souls' [Matthew v. 16] pp. 545-578.

*** In the British Museum copy some one has written (in pencil) 'Baxter: judicious, nervous, spiritual and remarkably evangelical tho' often charged to the contrary: a manly eloquence.'

XCII. Reasons for Ministers using the greatest plainness and seriousness possible in all their applications to their people. 1676. [8°].

*** I have not met with this. I suspect it was a 'Preface' or 'Epistle' to some book of another's. It is given by ORME in 'Practical Works,' Vol. XV.

XCIII. NAKED POPERY; or the Naked Falsehood of a book called the Catholick Naked Truth or the Puritan Convert to Apostolical Christianity: written by W.

H. Opening their fundamental errour of Unwritten Tradition and their unjust descriptions of the Puritan, the Prelatical Protestant and the Papist, and their differences; and better acquainting the ignorant of the true difference, especially what a Puritan and what a Papist is. By Richard Baxter, a Professor of meer Apostolical Christianity. London, Printed for N. Simmons at the Princes Arms in S. Paul's Church-yard. 1677 [4°].

Collation: Title-page — Treatise pp. 3-196—Contents pp. 7—Errata on reverse of last page.

*** My copy has on the title-page the autograph of 'B. Robinson' author of a treatise on 'Liturgies.'

XCIV. The Judgment of Nonconformists about the Difference between Grace and Morality. Printed in the year 1678 [4°].

Collation: Title-page—Errata on reverse—Treatise pp. 18.

*** This and the others onward, are stated in the 'Reliquiæ' [Part III. p. 185] to have been 'suppressed' which explains their great rarity.

XCV. The Death of Ministers improved or an Exhortation to the inhabitants of Horsley in Glocester-shire, and others, on the much lamented death of that reverend and faithful minister of the gospel Mr Henry Stubbs. By Tho. Vincent, John Turner, Rob. Perrot, M. Pemberton. To which is added a Sermon upon that occasion by Richard Baxter. Printed in the year 1678 [18°].

Collation: Title-page—the 'Address' as supra pp. 48—Then a separate title—'A Sermon preached at the Funeral of that holy, peaceful and fruitful minister of Christ Mr Henry Stubbs; about fifty years a successful Preacher at Bristol, Wells, Chew, Dursley, London, and divers other places. By his unworthy fellow-servant hasting after him, Richard Baxter. Printed in the year 1678.'

Title-page and Sermon pp. 54—[Text Acts xx. 24].

XCVI. Which is the True Church? The whole Christian World as headed only by Christ (of which the Reformed are the soundest part) or the Pope of Rome and his subjects as such? In three parts. I. The Papists Confusion in explaining the terms of the Questions: not able to bear the light. II. A Defence of a Disputation concerning the continued visibility of the Church of which the Protestants are Members. III. A Defence of the several Additional proofs of the said visibility. By Richard Baxter. Written especially to instruct the younger unexperienced scholars how to deal with these deceivers in these dangerous times. London, Printed, and are to be sold by Richard Janeway in Butcher-hall lane. 1679 [4°].

Collation: Title-page—Preface pp. 4—Treatise pp. 168—[At page 100 the pagination passes to 121 by misprint].

XCVII. The Nonconformist's Plea for Peace: or an Account of their Judgment in certain things in which they are misunderstood: written to reconcile and pacify such as by mistaking them hinder love and concord. By Richard Baxter. London, Printed for Benj. Alsop at the Angel and Bible over against the Stocks-Market. 1679 [8°].

Collation: Title-page—'To the reverend Conforming Clergy' pp. 10—Contents, etc. pp. 2—Treatise pp. 340—Errata 1 page—books pubd. by Alsop 1 page.
*** See 'Reliquiæ' [Part III. 180–187.]

XCVIII. A True Believer's Choice and Pleasure. Instanced in the Exemplary Life of Mrs Mary Coxe, the late wife of Doctor Thomas Coxe. Preached for her Funeral by Richard Baxter. London, Printed by R. E. in the year 1680. [4°].

Collation: Title-page—Dedication to Dr Thomas Coxe pp. 3—On reverse, Errata—Sermon pp. 65—[Text Psalm cxix. 111.]

XCIX. The True and only way of Concord of all the Christian Churches: the desirableness of it and the detection of false dividing terms. Opened by Richard Baxter. London, Printed for John Hancock at the Three Bibles in Pope's-head-alley over against the Royal Exchange in Cornhill. 1680 [cr. 8°].

Collation: Title-page—Texts etc. on reverse—the Preface 'To the honourable and reverend Dr George Morley, late Lord Bishop of Worcester and now of Winchester; and Dr Peter Gunning, Lord Bishop of Ely,' pp. 11—a Premonition pp. 7—Contents pp. 7—Errata 1 page—Pt. I. pp. 133—Pt. II. pp. 135-327—Pt. III. 144 [Text prefixed to Pt. I. Ephesians iv. 3.]

C. The Defence of the Nonconformists Plea for Peace or an Account of the Matter of their Nonconformity against Mr J. Cheney's answer called The Conforming Nonconformist and The Nonconforming Conformist to which is added the second Part in answer to Mr Cheney's Five Undertakings. By Richard Baxter. London, Printed for Benjamin Alsop at the Angel over against the Stocks-Market. 1680 [8°].

Collation: Title-page — the Preface pp. 6—Contents pp. 6—Treatise pp. 176.

CI. Fasciculus Literarum or Letters on Several Occasions.
 I. Betwixt Mr Baxter, and the Author of the *Perswasive to Conformity*. Wherein many things are discussed which are repeated in Mr Baxter's late Plea for the Nonconformists.
 II. A Letter to an Oxford

Friend concerning the Indulgence 167½.

III. A Letter from a Minister in the Country to a Minister in London.

IV. An Epistle written in Latin to the Triers before the King's most happy Restauration. By John Hinckley D.D. Rector of Northfeild in Worcestershire. London, Printed for Thomas Basset at the George near St Dunstans Church in Fleet-street. MDCLXXX. [8vo].

Collation: Title-page—Preface pp. 14 [unpaged] and pp. 344. The Baxter portion pp. 200.
⁎⁎* See 'Reliquiæ' [Part III. p. 90] for a short notice of Hinckley and his tactics.

CII. The Second Part of the Nonconformists Plea for Peace. Being an account of their Principles about Civil and Ecclesiastical Authority and Obedience (as far as the Author knoweth it) and about Things Indifferent, and evil by Accident or Scandal: and what their Nonconformity is not: and whether the Ministers encourage Sects and Schism: With their judgements and earnest desires of the Churches Peace and Concord, and the true and necessary means. Mostly written many years past, and now published to save our Lives and the Kingdom's Peace, from the false and bloody Plotters, who would first persuade the King and people that the Protestants, and particularly the Nonconformists are Presbyterians and Fanaticks; and next that it was such Presbyterians that killed his Father; and next that our Principles are rebellious; and next that we are plotting a rebellion and his death; and lastly that this is the genius of the Parliament; and therefore that they and we must be used as enemies to the King. By Richard Baxter.

London, Printed for John Hancock at the three Bibles near the Royal Exchange in Cornhill. 1680. [4°].

Collation: Title-page — The Preface pp. 22 [Signed R. e., no doubt a misprint for R. B.]—The Contents, etc. 'of this Extorted and Distorted Treatise' pp. 4 —Treatise pp. 204.
⁎⁎* No. LXXXVII. to LXXXIX. are often found along with this agreeably to 'Reliquiæ' [Part III. p. 188]. Orme enumerates them separately and as they were separately issued (though 'suppressed' afterwards) it seems right in this case to give each distinctly.

CIII. A Moral Prognostication. I. What shall befall the Churches on earth till that Concord, by the Restitution of their primitive purity, simplicity and charity. II. How that restitution is like to be made (if ever) and what shall befall them thenceforth unto the end in that golden age of love. Written by Richard Baxter. When by the King's Commission we (in vain) treated for Concord. 1661. And now published not to instruct the proud that scorn to learn; nor to make them wise who will not be made wise: but to instruct the sons of love and peace in their duties and expectations. And to tell Posterity that the things which befall them were foretold, and that the evil might have been prevented, and blessed peace on earth attained if men had been but willing, and had not shut their eyes and hardened their hearts against the beams of light and love. London, Printed for Thomas Simmons at the Princes Arms in Ludgate-street, 1680 [4°].

Collation: Title-page—To the Reader pp. 2—Treatise pp. 67.
⁎⁎* I have another edition 'London, Printed in the year 1680 and published in the year 1690 and are to be sold by Tho. Parkhurst at the Bible and three crowns in Cheapside near Mercer's

Chapel.' See 'Reliquiæ' [Part III. p. 188].

CIV. Church-History of the Government of Bishops and their Councils abbreviated. Including the chief part of the government of Christian princes and popes, and a true account of the most troubling controversies and heresies till the Reformation. Written for the use especially of them. I. Who are ignorant or misinformed of the state of the Antient Churches. II. Who cannot read many and great volumes. III. Who think that the universal Church must have one visible soveraign, personal or collective, Pope or General Councils. IV. Who would know whether Patriarchs, Diocesans, and their Councils, have been or must be, the cure of heresies and schisms. V. Who would know the truth about the great heresies which have divided the Christian world, especially the Donatists, Novatians, Arrians, Macedonians, Nestorians, Eutychians, Monothelites, etc. By Richard Baxter, a hater of false History. London : Printed by B. Griffin, and are to be sold by Thomas Simmons at the Princes Arms in Ludgate-street, and John Kidgell at the Atlas in Cornhill near the Royal Exchange. 1680. [4°].

Collation: Title-page — The Preface pp. 6—What history is credible and what not pp. 10: at end of page 10 'a notice concerning Mr Henry Dodwell'—Contents pp. 25—Books pubd. by Simmons 1 page—Treatise pp. 488.

CV. Richard Baxter's Answer to Dr Edward Stillingfleet's Charge of Separation : containing—
I. Some Queries necessary for the understanding of his Accusation.
II. A Reply to his Letter which denyeth a Solution.
III. An Answer to his Printed Sermon.
Humbly tendred I. To Himself ; II. To the Right Honourable the Lord Mayor and the Court of Aldermen ; III. To the Readers of his Accusation : the Forum where we are accused.
London, Printed for Nevil Simmons at the Three Cocks at the West-end of St Paul's, and Thomas Simmons at the Prince's Arms in Ludgate-street. 1680. [4°].

Collation: Title-page — The Preface pp. 5—and pp. 8-100—Appendix [unpaged] pp. 4.
⁎⁎ The Appendix is frequently awanting from ' Finis' being printed at close of page 100—a not uncommon thing with Baxter—for he has overflowing 'Postscripts' and 'Notes,' etc. etc. See 'Reliquiæ' [Part III. p. 187].

CVI. A Treatise of Episcopacy, confuting by Scripture, Reason and the Churches Testimony, that sort of Diocesan Churches, Prelacy and Government, which casteth out the primitive Church-species, Episcopacy, ministry and discipline, and confoundeth the Christian world by corruption, usurpation, schismes and persecution. Meditated 1640 when the etc. oath was imposed. Written 1671 and cast by : published 1680 by the call of Mr H. Dodwel, and the importunity of our superiors, who demand the Reasons of our Nonconformity. The designe of this book is not to weaken the Church of England, its government, riches, honour or unity : but to strengthen and secure it. 1. By the concord of all true Protestants who can never unite in the present impositions. 2. And by the necessary reformation of Parish-Churches, and those abuses which else will in all ages keep up a succession of Nonconformists. As an account why we dare not covenant by oath or subscription never to endeavour

Writings of Richard Baxter.

any (amending) alteration of the Church government (by lawful meanes, as subjects) nor make ourselves the justifying vouchers for all the unknown persons in the kingdom who vowed and swore it, that none of them are obliged to such (lawful) endeavours by their vow. By Richard Baxter, a Catholick Christian, for love, concord and peace of all true Christians, and obedience to all lawful commands of rulers; but made, called and used as, a Nonconformist. London, Printed for Nevil Simmons at the three Cocks at the West-end of St Pauls and Thomas Simmons at the Prince's Armes in Ludgate-street. 1681 [4°].

Collation: Title-page—Books of Baxter's pp. 2—the history of the production of this treatise, etc. pp. 10—Quotations 1 page—Contents pp. 3—Treatise—First Part pp. 170—Second Part pp. 233—Postscript pp. 3.

*** The Williams Library copy has manuscript [holograph] additions by Baxter. See 'Reliquiæ' [Part III. p. 188].

CVII. An Apology for the Nonconformists Ministry: containing I. The reasons of their preaching II. An answer to the accusations urged as reasons, for the silencing of about 2000, by Bishop Morley, Bishop Guning's chaplain, Dr Saywell, Mr Durel, the nameless Ecclesiastical Politician and Debatemaker the Counterminer, H. Fowlis, Dr Good, and many others. III. Reasons proving it the duty and interest of the Bishops and Conformists to endeavour earnestly their Restoration. With a Postscript upon oral debates with Mr H. Dodwell against his reasons for their silence. And a Scheme of Interests. Written in 1668 and 1669 for the most of it, and now published as an addition to the Defence against Dr Stillingfleet and as an account to the Silencers of the Reasons of our Practice.

By Richard Baxter. London, Printed for Thomas Parkhurst at the Bible and Three Crowns in Cheapside near Mercers Chappel. 1681. [4°.]

Collation: Title-page—Epistle Dedicatory to certain of the 'peaceful' Bishops pp. 6. Contents pp. 3. Treatise pp. 252. *** 'Reliquiæ' [Part III. p. 188.]

CVIII. Faithful Souls shall be with Christ: the certainty proved and their Christianity described and exemplified in the truly Christian life and death of that excellent, amiable saint Henry Ashurst Esq. citizen of London. Briefly and truly published for the conviction of hypocrites and the malignant, the strengthening of believers and the imitation of all, especially the masters of families in London. By Richard Baxter. London, Printed for Nevil Simmons at the Three Golden Cocks at the west end of St Paul's Church, 1681. [4°.]

Collation: Title-page—Epistle Dedicatory to widow and son pp. 6. Sermon [John xii. 26] pp. 60.

CIX. Poetical Fragments: Heart-Imployment with God and itself. The concordant discord of a broken-healed heart. Sorrowing-rejoycing, fearing-hoping, dying-living. Written partly for himself and partly for near friends in sickness and other deep affliction. By Richard Baxter. Published for the use of the afflicted. London, Printed by T. Snowden for B. Simmons at the 3 Golden Cocks at the west end of St Pauls. 1681. [18°.]

Collation: Title-page—To the Reader pp. 12 signed 'at the door of eternity' Aug. 7, 1681. Poems pp. 135. The three little volumes of Verse, by B. were collected together by the late celebrated Publisher Mr Pickering as the 'Poetical Fragments' of Baxter (1 vol. 12°) a very pretty and now scarce book.

CX. A Search for the English Schismatick: By the Case and

Characters I. Of the Diocesan Canoneers II. Of the Present Meer Nonconformists. Not as an Accusation of the former but a Necessary Defence of the later, so far as they are wrongfully Accused and Persecuted by them. By Richard Baxter, One of the Accused.
London : Printed for Nevill Simmons at the Sign of the Three Golden Cocks at the West-end of St Pauls Church-yard. 1681. [4°.]

Collation: Title-page. Postscript pp. 2. Treatise pp. 44.
⁎⁎* 'Reliquiæ'[Part III. pp. 188, 189].

CXI. A Third Defence of the Cause of Peace, proving 1. The need of our Concord 2. The Impossibility of it on the terms of the present impositions. Against the Accusations and Storms of viz. Mr John Hinckley, A Nameless Impleader, A Nameless Reflector or Speculum etc. Mr John Cheney's Second Accusation, Mr Roger L'Strange Justice etc. the Dialogue between the Pope and a Fanatic, J. Varney's Phanatic Prophesie. By Richard Baxter. London, Printed for Jacob Sampson, next to the Wonder Tavern in Ludgate-Street. 1681. [8°.]

Collation: Title-page—the Preface pp. 7.—books pp. 2. Answer to Hinckley pp. 128—to Cheney pp. 76. Impleader pp. 77–146. Reflector pp. 147–149—Varney and L'Strange pp. 150.

CXII. A Second true Defence of the meer Nonconformists against the untrue Accusations, Reasonings and History of Dr Edward Stillingfleet, dean of St Pauls etc. Clearly proving that it is (not sin but) duty. 1. Not wilfully to commit the many sins of Conformity. 2. Not sacrilegiously to forsake the preaching of the Gospel. 3. Not to cease publick worshipping of God. 4. To use needful pastoral helps for salvation, though men forbid it and call it Schism. Written by Richard Baxter, not to accuse others but to defend God's truth, and the true way of peace after near 20 years loud accusations of the silencing, prosecuting clergy and their sins. With some Notes on Mr Joseph Glanvile's zealous and impartial Protestant and Dr L. Moulins Character. London, Printed for Nevil Simons at the sign of the Three Golden Cocks at the West-end of St Pauls. 1681 [4°].

Collation: Title-page—an historical Preface pp. 10—a premised explication of the equivocal word 'church' pp. 4—advertisement at bottom of page—Contents pp. 4—Treatise pp. 195—books pubd. by Simmons.
⁎⁎* Able and acute as was Stillingfleet it only needeth to read this and No. CV. to be convinced of the larger and finer intellect of Baxter, as well as superior learning within the debated ground.

CXIII. A Breviate of the Life of Margaret, the Daughter of Francis Charlton of Apply in Shropshire Esq.; and Wife of Richard Baxter. For the use of all, but especially of their Kindred. There is also Published the Character of her Mother, truly described in her Published Funeral Sermon. Reprinted at her Daughter's Request, called 'The Last Work of a Believer, His passing-prayer, recommending his departing Spirit to Christ, to be received by him. London, Printed for B. Simmons at the Three Golden Cocks at the West-end of St Paul's. 1681. [4°].

Collation: Title-page—To the Reader pp. 8—'Breviate' pp. 107.
⁎⁎* Cf. John Howe's great Sermon, with loving and reverent 'Epistle' to Baxter, preached on the death of Mrs B. The 'Breviate' is very rare.

CXIV. An Answer to Mr Dodwell and Dr Sherlocke ; confuting

an Universal humane Church-supremacy, aristocratical and monarchical; as Church-tyranny and Popery: and defending Dr Isaac Barrow's treatise against it. By Richard Baxter, Preparatory to a fuller Treatise against such an Universal Soveraignty, as contrary to reason, Christianity, the Protestant profession and the Church of England: though the corrupters usurp that title. London: Printed for Thomas Parkhurst at the Bible and Three Crowns at the lower end of Cheapside near Mercer's Chapel. 1682 [4°].

Collation: Title-page—To the Reader pp. 10—Contents pp. 3—Letters between B. and Dodwell pp. 8—Treatise pp. 151 —Then separate title. 'An Account of my Dissent from Dr Sherlocke, his doctrine, accusations and argumentation. Especially about the essence of the universal, national and single Church, and the nature of Schism and the terms of Christian Concord. As also of my dissent from the French, from Bishop Gunning, and his chaplain Dr Saywell, Mr Thorndike, Bishop Bramhall, Bishop Sparrow, Mr Dodwell, etc., on the same subject. By Richard Baxter, not as their Accuser, but a Defender of himself and the Protestants against other mens accusations who call for the execution of the laws against us. London, Printed for Tho. Parkhurst at the Bible and Three Crowns in Cheapside near Mercers Chappel. 1681—pp. 155-230—books pp. 2.
*** See 'Reliquiæ' [Part III. p. 189.]

CXV. METHODUS THEOLOGIÆ Christianæ. 1. Naturæ rerum. 2. Sacra Scripturæ. 3. Praxi, congrua, conformis adaptata. Plerumque (corrigenda tamen et perficienda). Non 1. Ignavis, festinantibus, delassatis. 2. Stolidis, indocilibus. sectariis (ex homine et fuco judicantibus). 3. Superbis, mundanis, maliguis: Ergo, Non plurimis: Sed Juventutis Academicæ et Pastorum juniorum parti. 1. Studiosæ, sedulæ, indefessæ. 2. Ingeniosæ, docili, veritatem et ordinem sitienti. 3. Humili, can- didæ, Deo devotæ: Quippe ad 1. Veritatis indagationem, custodiam, propagationem. 2. Sanctitatis cultum incrementum laudem. 3. Ecclesiæ salutem, pacem, decus. Supra omnes natæ, disposita consecratæ. Dicata par Richardum Baxterum, Philotheologum.
Londini, Typis M. White et T. Snowden et prostant venales apud Nevil Simmons ad insigne trium gallorum in vico Ludgate prope Templium Paulinum. 1681 [folio].

Collation: Imprimatur, etc. on flyleaf — engraved title-page as *ante*,— Prefatio pp. 8 — Index pp. 12 — Postscriptum pp. 2—large circular engraving shewing the whole details—Treatise: Pars I. pp. 380—Pars II. pp. 381-450— Pars III. pp. 369—Pars IV. pp. 371-439.

*** 'This book cost him the most pains by far of any of his works. He was a great many years about it. It cost him one way or other about £500 [£2000 fully now] the printing: for he was forced to print it at his own charge. And after all 'tis generally esteemed so abstruse and scholastical that few have been willing to be at the necessary pains to understand it. But such as will excuse the Latin of it, will find a more than ordinary accuracy [of thought] in it. Calamy 'Account' Vol. I. p. 417. There can be no doubt that there are 'slips' in the Latinity of this 'Methodus' but it is an extraordinary book: and perhaps evidences more than any other the broadness of Baxter's intellect and the excursiveness of his speculation. There are too bits of terse, apophegmatic Latin worthy of Hobbes' renderings of Bacon: and there are separate 'Thoughts' that well translated would make a companion volume to Fuller's wise and quaint 'Thoughts:' without their sparkle but of perhaps a truer spirituality. See 'Reliquiæ' [Part III. pp. 69, 70] for a curious narrative of the preparation of this treatise.

CXVI. The Ready Way of comfuting Mr Baxter: a Specimen of the present mode of Controversie in England. On last page 'London, Printed for R. Janeway in Queen's-Head-Alley in Paternoster-row, 1682' [4°]—pp. 8. No title-page save *above*.

CXVII. The True History of Councils Enlarged and Defended, against the Deceits of a pretended Vindication of the Primitive Church, but indeed of the Tympanite and Tyranny of some Prelates many hundred years after Christ. With a Detection of the false History of Edward, Lord Bishop of Corke and Rosse in Ireland. And a Specimen of the way by which this Generation confuteth their Adversaries, in several instances. And a Preface abbreviating much of Ludolphus's History of Habassia. Written to shew their dangerous Errour, who think that a general Council or Colledge of Bishops, is a supream Governour of all the Christian World, with power of Universal Legislation, Judgment and Execution, and that Christ's Laws without their Universal Laws, are not sufficient for the Churches Unity and Concord. By Richard Baxter, a Lover of Truth, Love, and Peace, and a Hater of Lying, Malignity, and Persecution. To which is added by another Hand, a Defence of a Book, Entituled No Evidence for Diocesan Churches. Wherein what is further produced out of Scripture and ancient Authors, for Diocesan Churches, is described.

London, Printed for Tho. Parkhurst at the Bible and Three Crowns, at the lower end of Cheapside, near Mercer's Chappel. 1682. [4°].

Collation: Title-page — The Preface pp. 23—The Contents pp. 3—Treatise pp. 240—Defence of 'No Evidence,' etc.— Title-page and Errata on reverse— Preface pp. 6 and pp. 113—Postscript pp. 8.
*** 'Reliquiæ' [Part III. p. 189].

CXVIII. A Sermon preached at the Funeral of that faithful minister of Christ Mr John Corbet. With his true and exemplary Character. By Richard Baxter. London, Printed for Thomas Parkhurst at the Bible and three Crowns at the lower end of Cheapside. 1682. [sm. 4°].

Collation: Title-page—Sermon [from 2 Corinthians xii. 1-9] pp. 36, and 1 page giving list of C.'s writings.

CXIX. The Last Work of a Believer. His passing-Prayer, recommending his departing spirit to Christ to be received by him.
Prepared for the Funerals of Mary, the Widow first of Francis Charlton, Esq., and after of Thomas Hanmer, Esq.: and partly preached at St Mary Magdalens Church in Milk-street, London. And now, at the desire of her daughter, before her death, reprinted. By Richard Baxter.
London, Printed by B. Griffin for B. Simmons at the three Golden Cocks, at the West-end of St Pauls. 1682. [4°.]

Collation: Title-page—The Contents pp. 2—To the Reader pp. 12—Sermon pp. 79. [Text Acts vii. 29].
*** 'Reliquiæ' [Lib. I. p. 120].

CXX. Compassionate Counsel to all Young Men, especially I. London Apprentices. II. Students of Divinity, Physick and Law. III. The sons of magistrates and rich men. By Richard Baxter. London, Printed by T. S. and are to be sold by B. Simmons and Jonath. Greenwood at the Three Golden Cocks at the West-end of St Pauls and at the Crown in the Poultry. 1682 [12°].

Collation: Title-page—Contents pp. 2 —Treatise pp. 192.
*** Had an instant and sustained popularity: enormous numbers were gratuitously circulated. Not until '1691' did the Publishers put 'second edition' on the title-page—which edition contains a pretty full 'catalogue' of B.'s 'books' published and then unpublished—'Printed by H. Clark for George Conyers next door to the Princes Arms in Little Britain.' I have an edition of '1708' which has printed on the title-page 'the

gift of the Author'—'Printed for J. Luntley at the Three Bibles in Portugal-street near Lincolns-Inn-Fields.' See 'Reliquiæ'[Part III. p. 190].

CXXI. How to do good to Many: or the Publick Good is the Christians Life. Directions and Motives to it. Intended for an auditory of London citizens, and published for them, for want of leave to preach them. By Richard Baxter. London, Printed for Rob. Gibs at the Ball in Chancery Lane. 1682. [4°].

Collation: Title-page—'To the truly Christian merchants and other citizens of London' pp. 2—Treatise pp. 48. [Text Galatians vi. 10].

CXXII. Of the Immortality of Man's Soul and the nature of it and other spirits. Two discourses: One in a Letter to an unknown Doubter: the other in a reply to Dr Henry Moore's [More] Animadversions on a private Letter to him: which he published in his second edition of Mr Joseph Glauvil's Sadducismus Triumphatus or History of Apparitions. By Richard Baxter. London, Printed for B. Simons at the Three Golden Cocks at the West-end of St Pauls. 1682. [12°].

Collation: Title-page — the Preface pp. 6—Separate title 'The Nature and Immortality of the Soul proved. In answer to one who professed perplexing doubtfulness. By Richard Baxter. London [as before]—pp. 3-72. Separate title—'Of the Nature of Spirits: especially man's soul. In a placid collation with the learned Dr Henry More, in a Reply to his Answer to a private Letter, etc. [as before]—Letter [by Baxter to More] pp. 10—Treatise pp. 110.

CXXIII. The Catechizing of Families: a Teacher of Householders, how to teach their Households. Useful also to School-masters and tutors of youth. For those that are past the common small Chatechisms [*sic*] and would grow to a more rooted Faith and to the fuller understanding of all that is commonly needful to a safe, holy, comfortable and profitable life. Written by Richard Baxter, in hope that family and school-diligence may do much to keep up true Religion. London, Printed for T. Parkhurst at the Bible and Three Crowns at the lower end of Cheapside near Mercers Chappel, and B. Simmons at the Three Golden Cocks at the West-end of St Pauls. 1683. [8°].

Collation: Portrait 1674—Title-page—Reasons and use of the book pp. 10—Contents pp. 3—Errata and books pubd. 1 page—Treatise pp. 439—Books pubd. 1 page.
*** 'Reliquiæ' [Part III. p. 191].

CXXIV. Additional Notes on the Life and Death of Sir Matthew Hale, the late universally honoured and loved Lord Justice of the King's Bench. Written by Richard Baxter at the request of Edward Stephens Esq. the Publisher of his Contemplations and his familiar friend, and published by the urgency of others. London, Printed for Richard Janeway in Queens-head-alley in Paternoster-row. 1682. [12°.]

Collation: Title-page—To the Reader pp. 9—Note 1 page—Treatise pp. 45.

CXXV. A Continuation of Morning-Exercise Questions and Cases of Conscience practically resolved by sundry ministers in October 1682. London, Printed by J. A. for John Dunton at the sign of the Black Raven in the Poultry over-against the Stocks-market. 1683 [4°]. Serm. XI. 'The Cure of Melancholy and over-much sorrow by Faith and Physick' pp. 263-303. [Text 2 Corinthians ii. 7].

CXXVI. Obedient Patience in General; and in XX particular cases: with Helps to obtain and use it; and impatience repressed: Cross-bearers less to be pitied than

Cross-makers. Written for his own use under the cross, imposed at once by God and man, and published as now reasonable to many thousands who hold fast faith and conscience. By Richard Baxter. London, Printed for Robert Gibs, at the sign of the Ball in Chancery-Lane 1683. [12°.]

Collation: Title-page—the Preface pp. 6. Contents pp. 4. Treatise pp. 288.
⁎ Extremely rare and valuable as rare.

CXXVII. RICHARD BAXTER'S Farewell Sermon, prepared to have been preached to his hearers at Kidderminster at his departure, but forbidden. London Printed for B. Simmons at the Three Golden Cocks on Ludgate-Hill at the west-end of St Paul's. 1683. [4°.]

Collation: Title-page—To the inhabitants of K. pp. 2. Sermon [from John xvi. 22] pp. 42. [See LI.]

CXXVIII. Richard Baxter's Dying Thoughts upon Phil[ippians] i. 23. Written for his own use in the latter times of his corporal pains and weakness.

London, Printed by Tho. Snowden, for B. Simmons at the Three golden Cocks, at the West-end of St Pauls. 1683. [cr. 8vo.]

Collation: Portrait "Aetat 68" with Verses beneath—Title-page. The Preface to the Reader pp. 4. The Contents pp.16. Sentences on Love, Death etc. pp. 2. The Introduction [unpaged] pp. 16. Treatise pp. 259. Appendix pp. 260-357. Short Meditations on Romans v. 1-5, pp. 358-381.

CXXIX. Mr Baxter's Judgment and Reasons against communicating with the Parish-Assemblies, as by Law required. Impartially stated and proposed. Printed in the year 1684.

Collation: To the Reader pp. 6 and pp. 31. [See No. CXXXI.]

CXXX. Catholick Communion Defended against both Extreams : and Unnecessary Division Confuted, by Reasons against both the Active and Passive ways of Separation : Occasioned by the Racks and Reproaches of one sort, and the Impatience and Censoriousness of the other ; and the Erroneous, tho Confident Writings of Both. And written in Compassion of a Distracted, Self-tearing People, tho with little hope of any great success. In Five Parts.

I. The Dangerous Schismatick ; on the Three Cases about Church-Communion.
II. Animadversions on part of Mr Raphson's Book.
III. A Survey of the Unreasonable Defender. of Dr Stillingfleet, for Separation, pretending to oppose it.
IV. Reasons of the Author's censured Communion with the Parish Churches.
V. The Reasons why Dr J. O.'s Twelve Arguments change not his Judgement. By Richard Baxter, a Lover of Love and Peace ; and by defending them, displeasing those that labour to destroy them.

London : Printed for Tho. Parkhurst at the Bible and Three Crowns in Cheapside near Mercer's Chappel. 1684. [4°.]

Collation: Title-page—To the Reader pp. 3. The Contents pp. 3. A Separate title as follows : 'The Dangerous Schismatick clearly detected and fully confuted : for the saving of a distracted Nation from that which would destroy Christian love and unity. Occasioned by a Resolver of three Cases about Church-Communion. By Richard Baxter, a catholique Christian who is against confining Christian love and communion to any sect how great soever. London [as before]. Treatise pp. 58. Another title—' The Second Part against Schism' being Animadversions on a book famed to be Mr Raphson's. London [as before] —To the Reader 1 page. Treatise pp. 18. Another but no separate title (?)—the Preface pp. 44. A Survey of the Reply to Mr Humphrey and myself called a Vindication etc. of Dr Stillingfleet, pp.

56. Another but also without separate title 'Unnecessary separating disowned' in the reasons of the author's censured practice pp. 29. Then a separate title —'An account of the Reasons why the Twelve Arguments said to be Dr John Owen's change not my judgment about communion with Parish-Churches. By Richard Baxter. London [as before]— the Preface pp. 2. Treatise pp. 46. Postscript and Letter pp. 18—books pubd. by Parkhurst 1 page.

⁎ A perfect set, as above described, of this volume is exceedingly rare. See 'Reliquiæ' [Part III. pp. 197, 198]. ORME divides *above* into five distinct works in one place and other two in another.

CXXXI. Whether Parish Congregations be true Christian Churches and the Capable, Consenting Incumbents, be truly their Pastors or Bishops over their Flocks. And so Whether the old Protestants, Conformists and Nonconformists or the Brownists, were in the right herein. And how far our present Case is the same. Written by Richard Baxter as an Explication of some Passages in his former Writings; especially his Treatise of Episcopacy, misunderstood and misapplied by some; and answering the strongest Objections of some of them; especially a Book called

Mr Baxter's Judgment and Reasons against Communicating with the Parish Assemblies as by Law required. And another called, A Theological Dialogue.

Or Catholick Communion once more Defended upon men's necessitating importunity. By Richard Baxter.

London, Printed for Thomas Parkhurst, at the Bible and Three Crowns in Cheapside, near Mercer's Chappel, 1684 [4°].

Collation: Title-page pp. 2–43—Postscript 1 page—Answer to 'Theological Dialogue' pp. 30—Postscript pp. 31–32— [See No. CXXIX]. ORME makes *four* separate works of *above*.

CXXXII. Catholick Communion Doubly Defended: By Dr Owen's Vindicator and Richard Baxter. And the State of that Communion opened and the Questions discussed, whether there be any Displeasure at Sin or Repentance for it in Heaven. With a Parallel of the case of using a faulty Translation of Scripture and a faulty Lyturgy.

London, Printed for Thomas Parkhurst at the Three Bibles and Crown [as before] 1684 [4°].

Collation: Title-page — Preliminary 'Note' 1 page — Contents 1 page — Treatise pp. 40.

CXXXIII. The Judgment of the late Lord Chief Justice Sir Matthew Hale, of the nature of True Religion, the Causes of its Corruption and the Churches Calamity by mens Additions and Violences: with the desired cure. In three Discourses written by himself at several times. Humbly dedicated to the honourable Judges and learned lawyers who knew and honoured the author, because in their true sentiments of Religion and its depravations, and the cure, the welfare of England under his majesty, as well as their own, is eminently concerned. By the faithful Publisher, Richard Baxter. To which is annexed the Judgment of Sir Francis Bacon, Lord Verulam St Albans and Chancellour of England: and somewhat of Dr Isaack Barrow's on the same subject. London, Printed for B. Simmons at the three Cocks near the West-end of S. Paul's church, 1684 [4°].

Collation: Title-page—a Preface pp. 5—Contents pp. 5—Treatise pp. 64.

⁎ The 'Reliquiæ' contains various delightful notices of the great and good Judge.—See Part III. pp. 47, 175, 181.

CXXXIV. '*Unum Necessarium:* The One Thing Necessary or Christ's Justification of Mary's Choice and of his Servants wrongfully accused, 1685. Calamy: 'Account,' Vol. I. p. 420.

⁎ I have not met with this except in the re-prints *e.g.* in 'Practical Works' of Baxter, Vol. IV. pp. 759–781 [4 Vols. royal 8vo 1838]: also ORME, as before.

CXXXV. A Paraphrase on the New Testament with Notes doctrinal and practical by Plainness and Brevity fitted to the use of religious Families in their daily reading of the Scriptures, and of the younger and poorer sort of Scholars and Ministers who want fuller help. With an advertisement of difficulties in the Revelations. By the late Reverend Mr Richard Baxter. The second edition, corrected. To which is added at the end Mr Baxter's account of his Notes on some particular texts for which he was imprisoned. London, Printed for T. Parkhurst at the Bible and Three Crowns at the lower end of Cheapside: S. Sprint at the Bell in Little Britain: J. Taylor at the Ship, and J. Wyat at the Rose in St Paul's Church Yard. 1695 [8vo].

Collation: Portrait—Title-page—On reverse 'The Farewell' [poetry]—An Account of the Reason and Use of this Paraphrase pp. 4—the book not paged, final sheet E e e 2.—At the end An Advertisement respecting the difficulties in the Revelations signed 'Richard Baxter, London 1684, Nov. 12. Natali Authoris ætat suæ 70'—a Postscript pp. 8—On last page is 'Mr Baxter's own account of the cause of his imprisonment, left under his own hand to be printed with his Paraphrase.' Macaulay has made Baxter's 'trial' before Judge Jeffreys—for the 'Paraphrase,' etc. etc.—immortal.

CXXXVI. R. BAXTER'S Sence of the Subscribed Articles of Religion. London, Printed for Ben. Cox next door to the Dog-Tavern in Ludgate-street, 1689 [4°].

Collation: Half-title—and pp. 12—imprint at end.

CXXXVII. A Treatise of Knowledge and Love compared. In two parts I. Of falsely pretended knowledge II. Of true saving knowledge and love. I. Against hasty judging and false conceits of knowledge and for necessary suspension. II. The excellency of Divine love, and the happiness of being known and loved of God. Written as greatly needful to the safety and peace of every Christian and of the Church. The only certain way to escape false religions, heresies, sects and malignant prejudices, persecutions and sinful wars: all caused by falsely pretended knowledge and hasty judging, by proud ignorant men who know not their ignorance. By Richard Baxter who by God's blessing on long and hard studies hath learned to know that he knoweth but little, and to suspend his judgment of uncertainties, and to take great, necessary, certain things, for the food of his faith and comforts and the measure of his Church - Communion. London, Printed for Tho. Parkhurst at the Bible and Three Crowns at the lower end of Cheapside near Mercers Chapel. 1689. [sm. 4°.]

Collation: Title-page—Epistle Dedicatory to Sir Henry and Lady Diana Ashurst pp. 8. To the Reader pp. 2. Contents pp. 4. Treatise pp. 342. [Text 1 Corinthians viii. 2, 3.] books pubd by Parkhurst pp. 2.

CXXXVIII. Cain and Abel Malignity, that is, Enmity to Serious Godliness, that is, to an holy and heavenly State of Heart and Life: Lamented, Described, Detected and unanswerably proved to be the Devilish Nature and the Militia of the Devil against God, and Christ and the Church and Kingdoms, and the surest sign of a state of damnation. By Richard Baxter or Gildas Salvianus, who earnestly beseecheth all enemies, scorners, opposers and persecutors of serious Obedience to God, not to refuse so small a matter as the reading this short undeniable Evidence, to save their souls, while yet there is hope, from so damnable a state of Sin and Diabolism. Especially Magistrates and Clergymen, who are sacrilegious and blasphemous, if in the name of Christ's Ministers they turn those Sacred Offices against him. London, Printed for Tho. Parkhurst at the Bible and Three Crowns, at the lower end of Cheapside, near Mercer's Chapel. 1689. [12°].

Collation: Portrait — Title-page — To the Reader pp. 11 dated thus 'August 24. (1689) The fatal Day of Silencing in England in 1662.' Treatise pp. 146. See 'Reliquiæ' [Part III. p. 196].

CXXXIX. The Scripture Gospel defended and Christ, Grace and Free Justification Vindicated, against the Libertines, who use the names of Christ, Free Grace and Justification, to subvert the Gospel and Christianity, and that Christ, Grace and Justification, which they in zealous Ignorance think they plead for, to the injury of Christ, the danger of Souls, and the scandalizing of the weak, the insulting of Adversaries and the Dividing of the Churches. Yet charitably differencing the wordy Errours of unskilful Opiniaters, from their Practical Piety. And the mistaken Notions of some Excellent Divines, from the gross Libertine Antinomian Errours. In Two Books. The first, a Breviate of Fifty Controversies about Justification; written about thirteen years past, and cast by till now, after many provocations, by Press, Pulpit and Backbiting. The second upon the sudden reviving of Antinomianism, which seemed almost extinct near Thirty four years: And the re-printing of Dr Crisp's Sermons with Additions; with twelve Reverend Names prefixed for a decoy, when some of them abhor the Errour of the Book and knew not what was in it, but yielded by surprize only to declare that they believed him that told them that the Additions were a true Copy. By Richard Baxter, an Offender of the Offenders of the Church, by Defending the Truth and Duty which they fight against. London, Printed for Tho. Parkhurst at the Bible and Three Crowns at the lower end of Cheapside. 1690. [cr. 8°.]

Collation: Title-page — Texts pp. 5 and 'the Answer to all this by the Adversaries' 1 page.

There are the following separate titles—

(1.) A Breviate of the Doctrine of Justification, dilivered [*sic*] in many Books, By Richard Baxter: In many Propositions and the Solution of 50 Controversies about it. Written 1. To end such Controversies. 2. To confute rash Censurers and Errours. 3. To inform the Ignorant. 4. To procure Correction from wiser men, if I mistake. Occasioned by some mens accusation of me to others, that will not vouchsafe their instruction to myself. And by the Erroneous and dangerous Writings and Preachings of some well-meaning men, such as Mr Troughton etc. who at once mistake and misreport God's Word and ours, and fight in the dark against Christian Faith and Love.

London, [as before].

Collation: Separate title — The Preface pp. 5. The Prologue pp. 8. The Contents pp. 5. Treatise pp. 116.

(2.) A Defence of Christ and Free Grace: against the Subverters commonly called Antinomians or Libertines; who ignorantly blaspheme Christ in Pretence of extolling Him. In a Dialogue between an Orthodox Zealot and a Reconciling Monitor. Written on the Occasion of the reviving of those Errours and the Reprinting and Reception of Dr Crispes Writings, and the danger of subverting many thousand honest souls by the Notions of Free Grace and Justification misunderstood and abused by injudicious, unstudyed, prejudiced Preachers. By Richard Baxter. London [as before, but after Cheapside, is added 'near Mercers-Chapel.']

Collation: Separate title—To the Reader pp. 11. Another pp. 3. To the Teachers of Dr Crispe's Doctrine pp. 6. Treatise pp. 71. The Contents 1 page. Books published by Parkhurst 1 page. Extremely rare.

CXL. The English Nonconformity as under King Charles II. and King James II. Truly Stated and Argued. By Richard Baxter. Who earnestly beseecheth Rulers and Clergy, not to Divide and Destroy the Land, and cast their own Souls on the dreadful Guilt and Punishment of National Perjury, Lying, deliberate Covenanting to Sin against God, corrupt his Church and not amend, nor by Laws or blind Malignity, to reproach faithful Ministers of Christ, and Judge them to Scorn and Beggery, and to Lie and Die in Jails as Rogues, and so to strengthen Profaneness, Popery and Schism, and all for want of Willingness and Patience to Read and Hear their just Defence; while they can spend much more time in Sin and Vanity. The Author humbly begs that he and his Book of unconfutable Defence of a Mistaken persecuted Cause may not be Witnesses against them for such great and wilful Sin to their Condemnation. The Second Edition, Corrected and Amended.

London, Printed for Tho. Parkhurst at the Bible and Three Crowns, at the lower End of Cheapside. 1690 [4°].

Collation: Title-page. The Preface pp. 6. An Instance of the Accusations which call for our Defence etc. pp. 4. The Contents pp. 4. Treatise pp. 304.
*** On last page a pungent Note of the valiant old man, headed 'England's Slavery.'

CXLI. An End of Doctrinal Controversies which have lately troubled the Churches, by Reconciling Explication, without much Disputing. Written by Richard Baxter.

London, Printed for John Salusbury at the Rising Sun in Cornhil. 1691. [fc. 8°.]

Collation: Title-page—The Preface pp. 6—The Contents pp. 4—Books pubd. by Salusbury 1 page—Treatise, Preliminary chap. I. pp. xxxiv.—and pp. 320.
*** See 'Reliquiæ' [Part III. p. 182].

CXLII. The Glorious Kingdom of Christ, described and clearly vindicated against the bold asserters of a Future Calling and Reign of the Jews and 1000 years before the Conflagration, and the Asserters of the 1000 years Kingdom after the Conflagration. Opening the promise of the new heaven and earth and the everlastingness of Christ's Kingdom, against their debasing it, who confine it to 1000 years which with the Lord is but as one day. Answering Mr Tho. Beverley who imposed this task by his oft and earnest challenges of all the doctors and pastors, and his censure of dissenters as semi-Sadduces of the Apostasie in his Twelve Principles and Catechisms, etc. By Richard Baxter, whose comfort is only the hope of that kingdom. London, Printed by T. Snowden for Thomas Parkhurst at the Bible and Three Crowns, the lower end of Cheapside. 1691. [4°].

Collation: Title-page—to 'Mr Increase Mather, the learned and pious rector of the New England Colledge, now in London' pp. 2—Contents pp. 2—Treatise pp. 73—books pubd. by Parkhurst pp. 2.

CXLIII. The Certainty of the World of Spirits. Fully evinced by the unquestionable histories of apparitions, operations, witchcrafts, voices, etc. proving the immortality of souls, the malice and misery of the devils and the damned, and the blessedness of the justified. Written for the conviction of Sadduces and Infidels. By Richard Baxter. London, Printed for T. Parkhurst at the Bible and Three Crowns in Cheapside and J. Salusbury at the Rising Sun near the Royal Exchange in Cornhill. 1691 [cr. 8°].

Collation: Title-page — the Preface pp. 10—Contents pp. 4—Treatise pp. 246 — Postscript (though 'Finis' is on page 246) pp. 247-252—books pubd. by Parkhurst pp. 2 and pp. 2.
⁎⁎⁎ This as it is among the quaintest and most curious is also of the rarest of Baxter's writings.

CXLIV. A Reply to Mr Tho. Beverley's Answer to my Reasons against his Doctrine of the Thousand Years Middle Kingdom, and of the Conversion of the Jews. By Richard Baxter, passing to that world where we shall see face to face. Feb. 20, 169⅔. London. Printed for Tho. Parkhurst at the Bible and Three Crowns near Mercer's Chapel. 1691 [4°].

Collation: Title-page and pp. 21.
⁎⁎⁎ Among the least frequently met with of Baxter's tractates.

CXLV. Of National Churches: Their Description, Institution, Use, Preservation, Danger, Maladies and Cure : Partly applied to England.
Written by Richard Baxter for promoting peace when the pacifying Day shall come, by healing their extremes that are willing of Peace and Healing. And for the fuller Explication of the Treaty for Concord in 1660 and 1661 and of the Kings gracious Declaration about Ecclesiastical Affairs, for which he had publick thanks, by them that afterward rejected it. And for further Explication of his Treatise of Episcopacy and many others written for Peace and rejected.
London, Printed by T. Snowden for Thomas Parkhurst at the Bible and Three Crowns, the lower end of Cheapside. 1691. [4°].

Collation: Title-page—To the Reader pp. 3—The Contents 1 page—Books printed for Parkhurst pp. 2—pp. 72.

CXLVI. Against the Revolt to a Foreign Jurisdiction which would be to England its perjury, Church-ruine and Slavery. In two parts. I. The History of Men's endeavours to introduce it. II. The Confutation of all Pretences for it. Fully stating the Controversie, and proving that there is no sovereign power of legislation, judgment and execution over the whole Church on earth, aristocratical or monarchical, but only Christ's : especially against the Aristocratists who place it in a Council or College. By Richard Baxter, an earnest Desirer of the Churches concord, and therefore an enemy to all false terms and dividing engines and self-exalting sects ; and a Defender of Christ's own assigned terms which take in all the true Christians in the world and are injurious or cruel to none. To be offered to the next Convocation, beseeching them to own the doctrine of Foreign Communion but to note with renunciation the docrine of Foreign Jurisdiction and to vindicate the Reformed Church of England from the guilt and suspition which the French and innovators injuriously seek to fasten on them. London, Printed for Tho. Parkhurst at the Bible and Three Crowns at the lower end of Cheapside near Mercers Chapel. 1691. [8°].

Collation: Title-page—Epistle Dedicatory to 'Tillotson' then Dean of St Pauls pp. 7—To the Reader pp. 3—Contents of the first part pp. 2—Treatise pp. 366. The Second Part 'The Stating of the Controversie and full Confutation of the Pretences for a foreign jurisdiction' —Contents 1 page—Treatise pp. 369–552.

CXLVII. CHURCH CONCORD: containing I. A Disswasive from unnecessary division and separation and the real concord of the moderate Independents with the Presbyterians, instanced in ten seeming differences. II. The terms necessary for Concord among all true Churches and Christians. The first Part written 1655. The second Part 1667. And published this 1691. To second a late Agreement of the London Protestant Nonconformists: and a former treatise called The true and only terms of Church-Concord. By Richard Baxter. London, Printed for Tho. Parkhurst at the Bible and Three Crowns in Cheapside near Mercers Chapel, 1691 [4°].

Collation: Title-page — the Preface pp. 11—to the United Nonconformists in London pp. 2 — Contents 1 page — Treatise: Pt. I. pp. 59—Then a separate title as follows: 'Church Concord about Government and Order. The second Part. The just terms of agreement between all sober, serious Christians (by what names soever now distinguished:) in point 1. Of Catholick Communion: 2. Of particular Church Communion: 3. Of the Communion of neighbour Churches: 4. And of Churches of several kingdoms: 5. And of their duty as good subjects to their prince. Humbly offered to all the Christian Churches as the true and sufficient remedy of their divisions, if not rejected or neglected: and as a standing witness before God and man against dividing zeal and Church tyranny. By Richard Baxter, a servant of the God of love and peace. London [as before]'— To the Reader, dated 'Acton Nov. 21, 1688,' 1 page—Treatise Pt. II. pp. 62.

CXLVIII. Richard Baxter's Penitent Confession, and his necessary Vindication in answer to a Book, called the Second Part of Mischiefs of Separation, written by an unnamed author. With a Preface to Mr Cantianus D. Minimis in answer to his Letter which extorted this Publication. London, Printed for Tho. Parkhurst at the Bible and Three Crowns in Cheapside near Mercers Chapel, 1691 [4°].

Collation: Title-page—a Letter to Mr Baxter pp. 2—the Preface pp. 6—Treatise pp. 89—books by Baxter pp. 3.

CXLIX. The Protestant Religion truly stated: by the late Reverend Mr Richard Baxter. Prepared for the press some time before his death. Whereunto is added some account of the learned authors: By Mr Daniel Williams and Mr Matthew Sylvester. London: Printed for John Salusbury at the Rising Sun over against the Royal Exchange in Cornhill, 1692 [12°].

Collation: Title-page—To the Reader pp. 10—Contents pp. 3—Advt. of B's 'Life' on reverse of last leaf—Treatise pp. 185— Errata on page 185, before which it is said 'this book was delivered by Mr Baxter himself to the bookseller,' etc.—books pp. 3.

CL. The Grand Question Resolved, What we must do to be Saved. Instructions for a Holy Life. By the late Reverend Divine, Mr Richard Baxter. Recommended to the Bookseller a few days before his Death, to be immediately Printed for the good of Souls.

London: Printed for Tho. Parkhurst at the Bible and Three Crowns in Cheapside, 1692 [12°]

Collation: Title-page—and pp. 46.
*** This little treatise has been reprinted by me — It was unknown to Calamy and all the Bibliographers apparently. See my Prefatory Note.

CLI. Mr Richard Baxter's Paraphrase on the Psalms of David in metre, with other Hymns. Left fitted for the Press under his own hand. Licensed June 2d 1692. London, Printed for Thomas Parkhurst at the Bible and Three Crowns in Cheapside near Mercers Chappel: and Jonathan Robinson at the Golden Lion in St Pauls Church-yard. 1692 [12°]

Collation: Advertisement—Title-page —An Advertisement ['Epistle'] by Sylvester pp. 4—the Preface pp. 16—Paraphrase, etc. pp. pp. 273—Directions for the use and tuning of the Psalms pp. 274-276.

CLII. The Christian's Converse with God or the Insufficiency and Uncertainty of human Friendship and the improvement of Solitude in Converse with God: with some of the Author's breathings after him. By Richard Baxter. Recommended to the Reader's serious thoughts when at the house of mourning and in retirement. By Mr Matth. Silvester. London, Printed for John Salusbury at the Rising Sun over against the Royal Exchange in Cornhill. 1693 [12°].

Collation: Title-page—To the Reader pp. iii.-vii.—Contents pp. 2—books pp. 2 —Treatise [on John xvi. 52] pp. 167— books 1 page.

CLIII. Universal Redemption of Mankind by the Lord Jesus Christ: Stated and Cleared by the late Learned Mr Richard Baxter. Whereunto is added a short Account of Special Redemption by the same Author.

London, Printed for John Salusbury at the Rising Sun in Cornhill. 1694 [8°].

Collation: Title-page—Epistle Dedicatory to Foleys and Jolliff pp. 2 signed Joseph Read—To the Reader by Matthew Sylvester 1 page—Another by Joseph Read pp. 3—Treatise pp. 502— Books printed for Salusbury pp. 4 and Errata 1 page—See 'Reliquiæ' [Lib. I p. 123.]

CLIV. RELIQUIÆ BAXTERIANÆ: or Mr Richard Baxter's Narrative of the most Memorable Passages in his Life and Times.

Faithfully publish'd from his own original Manuscript by Matthew Sylvester. London, Printed for T. Parkhurst, J. Robinson, J. Lawrence and J. Dunton. 1696 [folio].

Collation: Portrait by White—Title-page—Epistle Dedicatory to Sir Henry Ashurst pp. 2—the Preface pp. 18— Contents pp. 6—Lib. I. Pt. I. and II. pp. 448—Part III. pp. 200—Appendix pp. 132.

$*_*^*$ Usually there follows Sylvester's Funeral Sermon for Baxter pp. 18— —Index pp. 8. To all who would possess themselves of a very jewel-case of original, penetrative, suggestive and affectionate criticism I commend COLERIDGE's Notes in the 'Reliquiæ' [Notes on English Divines pp. 5-119 edn. 1853.]

CLV. Poetical Fragments: Heart-Imployment with God and Itself. The concordant discord of a broken-healed heart. Sorrowing-rejoicing, fearing-hoping, dying-living. Written partly for himself and partly for near friends in sickness, and other deep afflication. By Richard Baxter. Published for the Use of the Afflicted. The third edition. London, Printed for Tho. Parkhurst at the Bible and Three Crowns in Cheapside Mercers-Chappel. 1699 [12°].

Collation: Title-page—To the Reader pp. 6—Poems pp. 158—books, etc. pp. 4.

CLVI. Monthly Preparations for the Holy Communion. By R. B. To which is added Suitable Meditations before, in, and after Receiving. With Divine Hymns in Common Tunes; Fitted for Publick Congregations or Private Families.

London; Printed for Tho. Parkhurst at the Bible and Three Crowns, the lower end of Cheapside. 1696 [18°].

Collation: Title-page—The Preface to the Reader by Matthew Sylvester pp. 8—Treatise pp. 172—Books pubd. by Parkhurst pp. 7.

CLVII. 'The Mother's Catechism or a Familiar way of Cate-

H

chizing Children in the Knowledge of God, themselves and the Holy Scriptures. 1701. 8vo. Calamy: 'Account' Vol. I. page 421.

₊ I have not been able to see this except in the modern reprints *e. g.* in Practical Works Vol. IV. pp. 34–64 [4 Vols. *royal 8vo.* 1838]: Preface by Sylvester.

CLVIII. Short Meditations on Romans v. 1–5.

₊ I have not seen this. It is given in 'Practical Works' 4 vols. royal 8vo. Vol. III. pp. 1063–1068]: also by ORME.

CLIX. OF REDEMPTION OF TIME.

₊ I have not met with this either. It is given as in CLVIII. [Vol. IV. pp. 1037–1042]: also by Orme.

☞ Both of these, as above, are taken from the original collected edition of the 'Practical Works' 4 vols. folio 1707: but are undated. I suspect they were 'Epistles' or 'Prefaces' to books by others.

CLX. and CLXI. I did not insert the following in their places because not having found either I am doubtful of their Baxterian authorship:—

(1.) The invaluable Price of an Immortal Soul. London. 1681. 8°.

(2.) Preparations for Sufferings: a Sermon. London. 1683. 8°.

These were once in Williams' Library: but have long been amissing. They appear in the Catalogue of 1841 [Vol. II.] *sub nomine.*

☞ ☜ As stated *ante:* ORME extends his List to 168 but this he does by repeatedly giving component parts of a treatise as independent. [See under Nos. III., CXXXI., etc. etc., in our List]. This he did as merely copying from Calamy or Book-Catalogues. He omits a number as well as inaccurately describes those included. We correctly describe *from actual copies* ALL given by him: and others unknown to him and other Bibliographers. 'Our Prefatory Note' explains that we hope to enumerate in a larger Work Baxter's 'Prefaces' or 'Epistles,' translations of his Writings, contemporary and later, the many volumes and tractates called forth in controversy with or concerning him, and of his Manuscripts. I have earnestly to request the co-operation of all lovers of Baxter in helping me to make this proposed supplement as complete as possible.

✝✝✝ Baxter like Bunyan repudiates various publications that took his name, *e.g.* 'Rules and Directions for Family Duties,' etc. etc. etc. A copy of these 'Rules' (a folio sheet) is in British Museum.

Crawford & M'Cabe, Printers, 7 George Street, Edinburgh.

Books by the
REV. ALEXANDER B. GROSART,
Prince's Road United Presbyterian Church, Liverpool.

I. ORIGINAL.

1. Small Sins. 3d edn., with additions, royal 16mo, cloth antique, price 1s. 6d., pp. 119.
2. Jesus Mighty to Save: or Christ for all the World and all the World for Christ. 3d edn., with additions, royal 16mo, cloth antique, pp. 204, price 2s.
3. The Prince of Light and the Prince of Darkness in Conflict: or the Temptation of Jesus. Newly Translated, Explained, Illustrated and Applied. Crown 8vo, pp. xxxiv. and 360, price 5s. [New and much enlarged Edition in preparation.]
4. The Lambs All Safe: or the Salvation of Children. 3d ed., with considerable additions, 18mo, cloth antique, price 1s.
5. Drowned: a Sermon in Memorial of the Death by drowning in Lochleven of Mr John Douglas. 3d edn. (3000) cr. 8vo, price 4d.
6. The Blind Beggar by the Wayside: or Faith, Assurance and Hope. 32mo, 4th edn., price 1½d. For enclosure in letters.

⁎ Translated into Effik by William Anderson, Old Calabar, W. Africa, 12°.

7. Joining the Church: or Materials for Conversations between a Minister and intending Communicants. 18mo, cloth antique, price 1s., 2d edn.
8. The Helper of Joy, 2d edn., 18mo, cloth antique, price 1s.
9. Recollections of Prayer-Meeting Addresses on Some of the Questions and Prayers of the Bible.
10. Thoroughness.
11. Tears or Consolation for 'The Poor in Spirit.'
12. Sundays at Sea: or What God says of the Sea and Sailors. [Nos. 9 to 12 in preparation].
13. Memoir of Richard Sibbes, D.D. 8vo (*See below*).
14. Memoir of Thomas Brooks, author of 'Precious Remedies,' etc. etc. 8vo (*See below*).
15. Memoir of Herbert Palmer, B.D. 8vo (*See below*).
16. Memoir of Henry Airay, D.D. (prefixed to reprint of his Commentary on Philippians). 4to.
17. Memoir of Thomas Cartwright, B.D. (prefixed to reprint of his Commentary on Colossians). 4to.
18. Memoir of John King, D.D., Bishop of London (prefixed to reprint of his Commentary on Jonah). 4to.
19. Memoir of John Rainolds, D.D. (prefixed to reprint of his Commentaries on Obadiah and Haggai). 4to.
20. Memoir of Richard Stock (prefixed to reprint of his Commentary on Malachi). 4to.
21. Memoir of Samuel Torshell (prefixed to reprint of his Exercitation on Malachi). 4to.
22. Memoir of Richard Bernard, B.D. (prefixed to his Exposition of Ruth). 4to.
23. Memoir of Thomas Pierson (prefixed to reprint of his Exposition of 'Select Psalms'). 4to.

Books by the Rev. A. B. Grosart.

24. Memoir of Samuel Smith (prefixed to reprint of his 'David's Blessed Man'). 4to.
25. Memoir of Richard Gilpin, M.D. (prefixed to reprint of his 'Demonologia Sacra'). 8vo.
   ₊ 100 large paper copies, with Portrait and fac-simile, price 15s. 6d.
26. Memoir of Michael Bruce (*See below*) author of 'Ode to Cuckoo,' 'Hymns,' etc.
27. Hymns. (*For private circulation*). Royal 32mo.

II. EDITED.

28. The Works, with Memoir, Introduction and Notes, of Richard Sibbes, D.D., Master of Katherine Hall, Cambridge, and Preacher of Gray's Inn, London. 7 vols. 8vo, £1, 11s. 6d.
29. The Works, with Memoir and Notes, of Thomas Brooks, 6 vols. 8vo, 25s.
30. The Works of Michael Bruce, with Memoir, Introduction and Notes. Cr. 8vo, 3s. 6d.
    ₊ Large paper edition, with numerous original Photographs, 10s. 6d.
31. The Works—with Memoir, Essay and Notes—of Robert Fergusson precursor of Burns. Cr. 8vo, 3s. 6d. (Portrait and Illustrations.)
32. Lord Bacon not the Author of 'The Christian Paradoxes.' Being a Reprint of 'Memorials of Godliness,' by Herbert Palmer, B.D.; with Introduction, Memoir, Notes and Appendix. Large paper, with Portrait, 8vo, 10s. 6d. 100 copies only: Small paper cr. 8vo, 3s 6d.: 250 *copies only.*
33. Selections from the Unpublished Writings of Jonathan Edwards, of America: with Introduction and Fac-similes. Royal 8vo, 7s. 6d. (300 copies only.)
34. The Grand Question Resolved—What must we do to be saved? Instructions for a Holy Life: by the late Reverend Divine Mr Richard Baxter. Recommended to the Bookseller a few days before his death, to be immediately printed for the good of souls. 1692.
    ₊ *Unknown to Biographers and Bibliographers*, cr. 8vo. [*See next*].
35. Annotated List of the Writings of Richard Baxter, author of The Saint's Everlasting Rest: made from Copies of the Books and Tractates themselves. Cr. 8vo. With No. 34, 3s. 6d: thick paper 5s.
36. The Poems and Translations in Verse (including Fifty-nine hitherto unpublished Epigrams, etc.) of Thomas Fuller, D.D., for the first time collected and edited, with Introduction and Notes. Cr. 8vo., 5s. 6d.: large paper (100 copies only) 10s. 6d.
    ₊ One of the 'Divine Poems' herein reprinted fetches in the book-market from £5, 5s. to £10, 10s., *i.e.* 'David's Hainous Sinne, Heartie Repentance, Heavie Punishment: another, the 'Panegyrick' on Charles II. from £2, 2s. to £3, 3s. Besides these there are all his Verses and Translations from his numerous prose Works, hitherto unpublished Epigrams, etc. etc. Printed for Private Circulation: *a limited edition.*
    ₊ Other privately printed Works of old Worthies, in *immediate preparation.*

London : JAMES NISBET & CO.   HAMILTON, ADAMS, & CO.
Edinburgh : WILLIAM OLIPHANT & CO.
Liverpool : ARCHIBALD FERGUSON, Bold Street.

www.ingramcontent.com/pod-product-compliance
Lightning Source LLC
Chambersburg PA
CBHW020153170426
43199CB00010B/1017